GRENADIER GRINS

Her Royal Highness The Princess Elizabeth
Colonel, Grenadier Guards
1942-1952

Photograph by Cecil Beaton

GRENADIER GRINS

To Brian and Maureen,
In friendship and admiration.
John.

Short, fun reminiscences of a life
associated with the Grenadier Guards
1956 to 2006

October 28, 2007

John Browne
Formerly Grenadier Guards

All profits from this edition donated to Grenadier Charities

Published June 2006

First Edition

Page and print design by Mel Abfier

Cover designed by John Browne

Published by John Browne
P.O. Box 408
Palm Beach, Florida 33480, USA

Printed and bound by Printwright, Ipswich, United Kingdom

International Standard Book Number: 0-615-13182-4

Library of Congress Number: pending

Dedication

To The Colonels-in-Chief, The Colonels,
Officers, Warrent Officers, Non-Commissioned Officers
and Guardsmen and also to the loyal Families
of the First or Grenadier Regiment of Foot Guards who
have contributed so much to the morale,
stability and freedom of our nation
over the past 350 years.

THE COLONEL-IN-CHIEF and THE COLONEL
of the First or Grenadier Regiment of Foot Guards
1997

Photograph by Lord Litchfield

Table of Contents

Grenadier Guards
1960's

Acknowledgements

In writing this book, I have relied upon personal recollection. However, I was assisted in refreshing my own meager memory by reference to those excellent journals *The Guards Magazine* and *The Grenadier Gazette*. My thanks go to the editors, my former brother officers and Sandhurst compatriots, Colonel Oliver Lindsay, OBE and Lieutenant-Colonel Henry Hanning.

I am greatly indebted to Susan Chopin who edited every line and whose ideas and suggestions provided a constant source of encouragement and the shielding of my appalling spelling.

I am most thankful to my former school study companion, Brigadier Christopher Bullock, OBE, MC, (60th KRRC), for advice and the use of photographs from his personal collection. Additional thanks are due to my former Squad Instructor at Sandhurst, Sergeant Edward Pittaway (Irish Guards), who kindly filled me with many memories and some photographs of our time at the Royal Military Academy.

I would like to express special thanks to some wonderful comrades-in-arms: Major Bob Woodfield, MBE, who kindly read the manuscript, and former Academy Sergeant Major Ray 'Flash' Huggins, MBE, MSM, with whom I shared many happy days in The Regiment, including playing rugby, and previewing the *James Bond* films that fortunately arrived in British Guiana early, before distribution to the rifle companies. Ray Huggins generously read the manuscript and whenever I telephoned him from America, without notice, he was invariably ready to assist in offering stories and advice in his characteristically energetic and good-humoured manner. One of my signallers, Quarter Master Sergeant Instructor Gerald Chamberlain, was of great assistance, providing memories of The Signal Platoon in BG, and his mother's letter about The Regiment.

I am especially grateful to Patrick Mc Sweeney, formerly Grenadier Guards, who most generously gave of his time and talent to create the cartoons.

Last, but not least, I would like to thank all those fine Grenadiers with whom I had the privilege and the enjoyment of both serving and knowing in later life. It is they who made this book possible and I salute them, one and all.

Office of
Alexander M. Haig, Jr.

February 22, 2006

John Browne

Dear John,

   As NATO Commander for a good part of the 70's, had I suspected that the Grenadier Guards were repeatedly involved in such shenanigans, international action might have been in order.

   Clearly your service with the Guards was great fun. For those who did not share your service, it constitutes a most enjoyable read. For those who did, additional fun is available.

                    Sincerely,

                    Alexander M. Haig, Jr.
                    NATO Commander
                    and 59th Sectretary of
                    State

Grenadier Guards
Drummer
1860

 *Introduction*

All nature wears one universal grin

—Henry Fielding

*P*ride in any organised body or group is a positive and valuable sentiment. That every soldier feels his regiment to be the best is good for all whom he serves.

Perhaps the three most significant qualities of any properly trained and well-led military organisation are courage, discipline and loyalty. Of these loyalty is the most important: loyalty to the Sovereign, the Commander or the Cause is the rock upon which morale is based. It is the fountainhead of the 'Winning Spirit' that can render even the smallest forces invincible and the stuff of legend.

As The Regimental Collect so rightly recalls, the heritage of the Grenadier Guards has proved a very costly one. It is fitting because history is filled with examples of the human cost of loyalty. Loyalty is the essence of nobility and true nobility is seldom cheap.

As a regiment of infantry the Grenadier Guards can never claim to be the most senior in the British army, yet none have shown more undivided loyalty to our Sovereign, nor fought more courageously. The seniority of the Queen's Colour over the Union Flag and the non-requirement to drink the Loyal Toast are fitting testimonies. What is more, this loyalty to and close association with the Sovereign shows clearly in the evolution of the Regimental title. Founded as 'The Royal Regiment of Guards' (1656); through the formation of the modern army (1660); to 'The King's Regiment of Foot Guards' (1665); to 'The

First Regiment of Foot Guards' (1685); and on to its present title, 'The First or Grenadier Regiment of Foot Guards' (1815).

The wearing of the 'elite' bearskin cap by the entire Regiment and the addition of the word 'Grenadier' to the title commemorated The Regiment's distinguished performance, and severe depletion, at *Quatre Bras*, the crossroads connecting the opposing forces of Wellington and Napoleon. On the following day, outside Waterloo, The Regiment's steadiness under sustained artillery bombardment and five massive French cavalry charges culminated in the epic defeat of key elements of the Emperor's Imperial Middle Guard. Witnessing *La Garde* retreat for the first time in its history, the French army turned from a formation into a crowd, and defeat was visible. Wellington, having been in the square of the 2nd Battalion, First Guards for the cavalry attacks, then ordered the General Advance. The Old Guard remained the only formation to cover Napoleon's retreat. Europe was saved.

This title of 'Grenadier' represents the only example of a British regiment having won its official title in battle. The award of 80 battle honours is testimony that The Regiment has displayed decisive courage, discipline and heroic example in many theatres of war since Tangier in 1680.

The Regiment has provided much of the foundation stock of other fine regiments, and Grenadiers have consistently held senior appointments at the Royal Military Academy, Sandhurst, and elsewhere. With such a pedigree who can disagree with the heartfelt sentiment expressed to me by a former First World War veteran and King, Edward VIII, later Duke of Windsor, who said of the Grenadiers, "They're the Best of the Best...Yes, ...the Best!"

My first interviews to gain entry to The Regiment took place in 1956. My chief sponsor was Lieutenant-Colonel Charles Earl, DSO, OBE (formerly, Adjutant at Sandhurst). The Colonel of The Regiment was General the Lord 'Ma' Jeffreys, KCB, KCVO, CMG, who saw distinguished service in both World Wars. In 1915, as Commanding Officer of the 2nd Battalion, he earned the battalion the front-line trench accolade of *elite*. The subsequent nickname was 'The Models'. On his last mounted Queen's Birthday Parade I remember seeing him, legs weakened, held on his horse by his neighbouring non-Royal Colonel, Field Marshal The Earl Alexander of Tunis (Irish Guards, and another veteran of both world wars). As the pair followed the Queen back from the 'Inspection' the Field Marshal, dressed in slippery Foot Guards woollen overalls, with none of the 'grip' of leather breeches or high boots, held the Colonel by the arm. Astride a hard, polished military saddle he risked his own seat and a bad, sensational fall on a State Occasion. To see these two old 'war horses' limping into port under the Horse Guards arch was a fine example of helping out a comrade-in-arms (not under the hail of enemy fire this time, but the full glare of television cameras) and characteristic of veterans of the First World War, and of the Household Division.

The Lieutenant Colonel of The Regiment was Colonel Sir Thomas Butler. Baronet, DSO, OBE (afterwards Her Majesty's Lieutenant Governor of the Tower of London). The Regimental Adjutant was, if memory serves, Major David Fraser, (later General Sir David, GCB, OBE, former Commanding Officer of the 1st battalion and Vice Chief of the Defence Staff). He was succeeded by Major Sir Hugh Hamilton-Dalyrymple, Baronet, (subsequently GCVO, and in charge of The Queen's Body Guard for Scotland, the Royal Company of Archers).

As a schoolboy, it was indeed awe-inspiring to be interviewed by such men as these. My Father gave me a ticket to the Queen's Birthday Parade and my wonderful housemaster, John Farebrother, whose brother was a Grenadier, gave me an *exeunt* day. I saw a tall, very smart and Honourable Jeremy Monson Troop the 3rd Battalion Colour as the Ensign (whether by coincidence or planning, Jeremy's kinsman, Captain John Monson, was given command of a company in Lord Wentworth's Regiment when it was formed by King Charles II in 1656, 300 years beforehand).

The Regiment was abuzz with the Tercentenary Celebrations, with much praise given to Major David Fraser for creating a superb theatre *collage* of The Regiment's 300 years of history. For me, the recruiting 'fly' looked superb. I bit down on the hook and never regretted it. For many of us, the Grenadier Regiment was far more than a regiment; it was a way of life for Guardsmen and Generals alike.

It was a privilege to serve for a few happy years in the 'human river' that is the Grenadier Guards, during part of its illustrious 350-year passage through British history. We trained hard and regularly for war, yet never experienced high intensity operations. Ours was the era of nuclear deterrence, overshadowed by the threat of mass mutual destruction. Therefore, there are no war stories to tell. However, we did have public duties to perform and we did have fun. Much of our fun was irresponsible but, with the threat of total annihilation, why not? I hope the passage of time will be kind and not drag me out of exile in America to face the 'Green Door' to account for any of my misdeeds!

Most Grenadiers have served in a thoroughly gallant and creditworthy manner and many may have experienced far more important, heroic and amusing scenes. This is the record of just some of the (printable) events that occurred in the junior footprints of a sometimes scruffy and often idle young Grenadier. It contains repitition as each story was designed to stand alone. It may also contain some 'confusing' American spelling! Some may feel that it constitutes an account that is too autobiographical – with repeated use of the word 'I'. I have no answer, save to paraphrase Tom Wolfe who once, when faced with the same charge, replied, "it is based upon personal experiences, most already distant and I ask, what are we but the sum of all the moments of our lives?" This account will not inspire, but I hope that it may amuse and, perchance, cause some grins.

Part One

You're in the army now
You're not behind the plough
You son of a bitch you'll never grow rich
You're in the army now
—unknown

THE GUARDS DEPOT, CATERHAM

Anyone who entered the imposing main gate of the Guards Depot at Caterham has an indelible image etched into his personal 'hard-drive' memory.

I believe that most of those who passed through the old Guards Depot would agree that it is almost an understatement to say that Caterham was extreme!

My parents and my sister dropped me off outside the gate. Thanks to Malvern contemporaries and masters, who had already trodden the potential officers' Brigade Squad path, and anxious to seem equal to the occasion, I addressed the fierce Sergeant of the Guard as 'Sergeant', thus reducing the risk of a verbal explosion. However, contrary to official instructions, my suitcase was heavy, making yet more excruciating the march to the Medical Inspection (MI) room, at around 200 paces to the minute, behind a fit young drummer. On the long march I was threatened with the cells for idle marching by Grenadier Drill Sergeant Tom Pugh. (I was innocent enough to think the cells were reserved for criminals but soon learned differently).

Inside the MI room I met fellow squad members and those from the Household Cavalry, looking apprehensive but smart in their new uniforms issued beforehand at Windsor.

On the introductory parade, we were formed into lines outside the MI room, still in plain clothes and carrying our heavy suitcases, before being divided into two regimental squads. The first squad was made up of Life Guards, Blues, Grenadiers and Welsh Guards, under Sergeant A. Dunks (Grenadier Guards). The Coldstream Guards, Scots and Irish Guards, under Sergeant Torrance (Scots Guards), comprised the second squad. The senior Sergeant, Dunks, opened proceedings by announcing, "Right! Now, we want to see that the Blue blood content of this squad is up to normal Brigade standards. "Any Princes, put your hands up!" No one moved. "What, no Royalty? Not a very good start for you lot. There'd better be a lot of 'ristocrats among you, to make up for this deficiency in Royals!" Having run the gamut of Dukes, Marquises, Earls, Viscounts, 'ordinary' Peers of the Realm and even Baronets, he added, "Well, now let's get down and really scrape the dregs from this shower. Any Honourables here?" A smattering of hands went up. Advancing abruptly upon the Honourable Nicholas Cunliff-Lister (Welsh Guards), near the centre of the front rank, he bent over to place his nose just fractions of an inch from Cunliff's face before yelling out "You 'orrible 'common' little man!"

After we had been divided into two squads, Sergeant Dunks set about the first stages of familiarising himself with our faces. He had a certain difficulty, or pretended to have, over the Marquis of Dufferin and Ava.
"And what's your name then?"
"Dufferin and Ava, Sergeant."
"Dufferin *and* Ava? What have we here, a man with two f****** names, one for odd days and one for even days? Don't

you dare think you can take the Mickey out of me! You're either Dufferin or you're Ava. You can't be both. Your just f****** Dufferin, understand?"

In the space of a few days we had shed the lives of schoolboys. Gone were our morning tailcoats, silver-topped canes, 'bashers' (or boaters), private fagables and the youthful arrogance that sometimes accompanies massive authority, including the spot delivery of corporal punishment. Power and privilege were consigned to the past with our plain clothes. We were in the army now, dressed in ill-fitting denims, draws cellular, tin hats and new boots. Each of us had crew-cut hair, a hus'ife (housewife or sewing kit) and a rifle. We were armed not with a cane but with Brasso. Any spare moments were spent sitting astride our beds, cleaning and re-cleaning kit. Our first fatigues included cleaning round the latrines with our eating forks. If any recruit broke his fork, Trained Soldier Williams was on hand to provide a replacement, at a price.

We were the lowest of the low. Even the dog that padded past our lines could walk. For us everything, but everything, was done at the double and usually to a fanfare of shouted encouragement. We were sworn at continuously. Indeed, it was at Caterham that I heard my first sentence composed entirely of swear words. Actually, it was the same word, or derivative thereof. Trained Soldier Savage (Irish Guards) had sought leave to 'fall in' to our hut from our squad instructor, Grenadier Sergeant Dunks. Permission was granted. Savage, turning smartly to his right, put his left foot down so hard that it went through the floorboards. The mono-worded sentence was a fusillade and carried a certain distinctive flavour: 'F******, f******, f******, f***!'

As this suggests, life at Caterham was rigid. Perfect was the only recognised standard. Discipline was harsh, sometimes even brutal. Pace sticks were not used merely to measure the pace. A well-aimed blow from one was literally crushing to the unfortunate recipient. On one occasion a hapless drummer who failed in a suicide attempt using his bootlaces was charged, not with 'misuse' but with 'idle' use of military equipment. Of course, it was shocking. But then Caterham was shocking. Indeed, I doubt that the man lives who was not at sometime taken aback by life as a recruit at the depot.

A Trained Soldier, whom all recruits found formidable, held sway over the daily lives of recruits assigned to his 'care'. Non-commissioned Officers were 'Princes', Warrant Officers 'Kings' and Officers 'Emperors' in the eyes of most recruits. Amongst the Grenadier staff in 14 Company when I passed through Caterham were Major Warren Freeman-Attwood, Captain (The Duke) Guy Ellerington (formerly Guards Parachute Company), and Lieutenants David Davenport and the Honourable Jeremy Monson. The Sergeant Major was Fred Clutton MM, the senior Drill Sergeant Tom Pugh, the Company Sergeant Major Ray 'Flash' Huggins, and the Pay Sergeant, Sid Dowland BEM (former SAS, and Special Boat Section during the Second World War), Sergeant G. Nash was permanently attached to the Brigade Squad and the superintending Gold Sergeants included Sergeants A. Dunks, Sharman, Gilman and R. Brown (weapon training staff).

A distinct sub-atmosphere of fear existed: the fear of failure, of being singled out as idle, or of letting down the team, and of brutality. The cry "take his name" caused shivers, and the smallest speck of dust or even suggestion of a foreign body was an offence. Lateness, defined as a failure to be five minutes early, was never tolerated. The only moments of daytime relaxation were Church Parade, Padre's Hour, representative sport and the strictly rationed 'reward' of time in the NAFFI, listening to popular tunes such as 'Diana' and 'Tammy'; or of deep reflection in the cells. Any time spent 'resting' in the latter had a painful and highly predictable price.

Yet for the majority of recruits, the 'Caterham experience' prepared guardsmen for the extreme mental and physical shocks, strains and deprivations which are the unfortunate hallmarks of high intensity war. Sadly, for a few vulnerable souls, this was all too much. It was a dreadful and unacceptable price to pay in peacetime, post-war Britain.

In Autumn 1957 an acute attack of Asian flu struck the

Guards Depot. A number of recruits died needlessly, some possibly because they were chased as 'malingerers'. Some were those who merely pretended to drink the regulation amount of water on water drinking parades. Doctors believed quantities of water limited the worst effects of the outbreak and we were ordered to drink flagons of water by numbers. I witnessed the fatal effects of one Guardsman 'cheating' on water-drinking parade. Upwards of 1,500 men were down at one time, confined to barrack blocks converted into temporary hospital wards. One of our Medical Officers was Doctor Roger (later Sir Roger) Bannister, one of the leading members of a vintage post-war sporting generation (of whom more later).

Life at Caterham following the flu epidemic changed dramatically. The food improved immeasurably and, significantly, discipline became far less harsh. Overnight Caterham entered the post-war era. The speed with which these fundamental lifestyle changes were accomplished illustrated well the unquestioning obedience of the Household Brigade (as it was then). It also enabled the Brigade to deal with its own peacetime survival by recruiting volunteers, following the abolition of National Service (conscription).

Against this background we had entered the Space Race, the Soviet Union launching the world's first spacecraft, Sputnik 1. It was a serious blow to learn that the Soviets had beaten the West to the vital ground of any future strategic war – Space – and prompted the Americans to establish NASA. Trained Soldier Williams (Welsh Guards) allowed us the rare privilege of listening to the 'bleep, bleep, bleep' signal, and to the astonished world commentary, on his wireless set. The Russian spacecraft in orbit seemed to signify the dawning of a new age in a sharply changing world.

As transition to military life took hold, the sense of fear, deprivation and harshness of Caterham, was gradually overcome in the minds of most recruits. It was replaced by a deep sense of self-respect and confidence, tempered with a humility that enabled Guardsmen both to respect others and, in turn, to earn respect. This self-respect, combined with a

Right Mental Approach, enables Guardsmen not just to believe in themselves but, as part of a team, beyond themselves. It is also this basic self-respect, called pride by some, that ensures the survival of Guards standards, even where no supervision exists. This, in turn, leads to ingrained obedience and to the maintenance of operational efficiency and loyalty under extreme conditions and sets Guardsmen apart. It was this self-respect that resulted in no Guards formations returning from Dunkirk in 1940 without their rifles. Even in retreat, Guards formations did not tramp or walk, they marched. Such example instilled essential morale in others.

As recruits, we found almost all instructors intolerant and of alarming vigour and ferocity. Yet in fact, upon meeting them subsequently in battalion life, we discovered the most benevolent of men. Officers, Warrant Officers and Non-Commissioned Officers of the Household Brigade were the very ablest of men, concentrating upon two factors vital to long-term success - the care and training of their men.

Explanatory note:
"Losing one's Name" seems to have originated from kit inspections. Full kit was laid out on one's bed, immaculately blancoed, polished and folded, according to a rigid plan. Often this kit was inspected in one's absence. If it did not measure up, the inspecting Officer or Non-Commissioned Officer would cry out "Take his name!" As quick as a flash, the poor unfortunate's shining brass name plate would be taken from his bed and held ready for the compilation of a list of those due to face the 'Green Door' of the Company Commander's office.

Chapter 1

"You! Take That Grin off Your face!"

The Guards Depot, Caterham, Autumn 1957

"You! Take that grin off your face!" barked Sergeant Dunks, pointing his pace stick at me threateningly. Our Brigade Squad had 'got on parade' and we were assembled in ranks to the right of 14 Company, Grenadier Guards, waiting for the order to 'form up.'

"I see him, Sergeant Dunks. Take his name, 'grinning' on parade!" bellowed Sergeant Major Fred Clutton, MM. the finest of Grenadiers who earned his Military Medal heroically as a Lance Sergeant in The King's Company during the Second World War. He was a towering figure, who was a good 40 yards away, 'marching the ground' in the awesome company of Drill Sergeants Pugh (Grenadier Guards) and Morse (Coldstream Guards).

"Got 'im, Sir, 'grinning on parade, Sir," echoed Sergeant Dunks. His look was dominating. The eyes had it.

"And while you're there Sergeant Dunks, the left hand man, front rank," roared Fred Clutton, "He's moving his eyes about!" This unfortunate target was Michael Moore, another Grenadier recruit, son of Major General Sir Rodney Moore, former Commanding Officer of the 2nd (tank) battalion of the Grenadier Guards from Normandy to Germany in World War Two, then Commanding London District and, subsequently, General Sir Rodney GCVO, KCB, CBE, DSO, for whom I acted as an 'Esquire' in the Order of St John. He had so many orders (including foreign) and campaign medals that in the Autumn of his days, profusely decorated, and leading the 2nd Battalion on Regimental Black Sunday (Remembrance) Parades, he appeared literally to be bent over by their weight.

"Got 'im, Sir, 'moving his eyes about on parade, Sir!" replied Sergeant Dunks. It was hard to see our eyes, at six feet, let alone at 40 yards, under the peaks of our khaki forage caps. However, that was Caterham. We felt that we would all visit the guardroom cells, at least once, before we passed out. It was, after all, an excellent way in which to acquaint potential officers with the true rigours of the punishments they might in future be required to administer to men under their command.

A moment or two later, the Adjutant (Captain Harrison, Scots Guards) called out, "Form up, Sergeant Major."

"Sir!" replied Fred Clutton, setting in motion a time-honoured series of routines. All the Non-Commissioned officers were inspected by the Adjutant, in front of the men - no favours at Caterham! Everyone, but everyone, had to be perfectly turned out. The routine culminated with "call the role" which heralded the 'Caterham Howl' as scores of squad instructors got a 'grip' of their squads.

Sergeant Dunks did not have much time to 'grip' us, for Fred Clutton's blood was up. Following the opening formalities of the parade he strode purposefully over to our squad shouting "Alright Sergeant Dunks, I'll take over. This looks like a squad that needs waking up. I'll teach them to grin on parade and move their eyes about!" A major 'rifting' followed. It became something of a showpiece for the rest of the parade, demonstrating just how a good 'rifting' (repeated drill exercises at a very rapid pace) should be conducted. It certainly provided an example of what to expect if a squad member aroused the Sergeant Major's wrath. One of us, Willie Pryor (Welsh Guards), was put in close arrest and doubled off to the cells, for 'idle marking time.' It was classic Caterham. The squad was only as good as the weakest link, whether it was in cleaning kit, drill or during weapon training. I believe that was and remains a major ethos behind the vital team spirit (*Septum in Juno*) that has rendered the Household troops so flexible, team-orientated and effective in war.

I admit that the merest suggestion of a smile may have crossed my face. Just moments before, I had been approached by another Grenadier legend, Company Sergeant Major Ray 'Flash' Huggins (subsequently MBE, MSM - the Meritorious Service Medal was awarded to only 100 men in the entire army and carrying a gratuity of... wait for it... ten pounds!) An experienced Army rugby player, Ray Huggins was later to be a powerful ally in running our undefeated 2nd Battalion rugby side. He went on to be Academy Sergeant Major at Sandhurst and, as such, the senior Warrant Officer in the British Army. Immaculately smart, I had heard him approach me from 14 Company during the deathly hush that preceded the explosive action of all parades at Caterham. He stood behind me menacingly, pace stick in hand. I trembled, speculating on what could have possibly directed the steps of such a senior person towards little me on this vast parade of over 1,500 men (614 in 14 Company alone). In a staged whisper he growled authoritatively in my left ear, "You're playing rugby for the Guards Depot at three o'clock tomorrow afternoon. Don't be late! Understand?"

'Sir!" I replied with both relief and glee, possibly accompanied by the hint of a smile. Sadly, my feelings of pleasure were not well enough camouflaged from the eagle eye of Sergeant Dunks, who was watching intently at this apparent interference in 'his' Brigade Squad.

Well, rugby was far more than a game at Caterham, it promised two of the rarest of commodities - almost two hours of mental relaxation, and the luxury of a shower in one's own time. Normally, sweating all day, we were allowed only two showers a week, of five minutes duration. Our squad instructor would parade us in denims and boots (later we graduated to the privilege of gym shoes), alongside other waiting squads, outside the bathhouse. When our allotted time came he would release 30 of us, all battling to get though a narrow doorway. Slipping and sliding on the concrete in our studded boots we tried to find a vacant shower and adjust the outdated water controls. Often, just as we had lathered up, our instructor would call out, "One minute! I don't want anyone to have to spend the rest of the night in the cells for being late! Come on, out! Thirty-five seconds; thirty-four..." Whatever our state of dryness, boots and denims were forced on again with difficulty as we ran, skidding to a halt in the ranks outside. It does not take much to imagine the joy of a shower, *in one's own time*. (It is a joy I relish to this very day, some fifty years later, when dipping my toe ever so gently into a steaming bath).

I no longer recall the result of the match, but I do remember basking in the luxury of an individual shower when, with a great crash, the bathhouse door was abruptly kicked open, totally shattering my moments of bliss. Two Irish Guards Trained Soldiers appeared with some forlorn recruit and bundled him into a shower, flinging a large bar of army regulation soap at him. He gasped as it hit home. Then, brandishing giant floor brushes, one of his tormentors shouted, "We'll teach you to have 'dirty flesh' on an officer's foot inspection!" (This may have been the smallest speck of black, or of grey sock-wool, under a toenail). "We'll give you a scrubbing you won't forget!" The cries curdled my blood. It was time to leave and fast.

At Caterham, recruits were reasonably 'safe' when in a squad under an instructor, jealous of his command. In the Brigade Squad our instructors were Gold Sergeants and the only people inclined to turn their attention on us were Company Sergeant Majors and above. Such 'Kings' were a rare sight, thank God. A recruit was generally at his most vulnerable when alone, as often in war. A lone recruit, particularly a 'toff' from the Brigade Squad, represented an inviting target for any prowling junior Non-Commissioned Officer or Trained Soldier. In common with many armies they were often vicious. It was vital for me to get out of that bathhouse without being spotted or I may have been 'invited' to join the 'scrubbing party' and probably still bear the scars. It was a 'built-up-area' situation, but I used my limited knowledge of field craft to get away sharpish and back to the relative sanctity of our squad hut.

Chapter 2

Heroes All

The Brigade Squad messed with 5 Company Irish Guards, the Micks, close to our lines. Food, an ever absorbing topic, was abysmal, even worse than at school, at least until the Asian flu epidemic struck. That said, it was food and we were very active and extremely hungry. We ate everything we were given. In fact, we were all so hungry that some Mick recruits would not overly concern themselves over the knifing of meat or even a potato from a nearby plate, particularly the plate of a 'pansy' Brigade Squad neighbour. In response, we would try to sit in clusters of our own squad, leaving only the 'flanker' members exposed, defending their plates from only one side. All this changed on one memorable day.

William Wykeham, Bishop of Winchester, instituted the Public School system some 627 years ago. He syndicated the costs amongst parents. The schools were indeed open to the public, so long as they could afford to pay their share of the syndicated fees. These so-called Public Schools have long been richly denounced for buggery, bullying and beating. Yet for many years boarding schools provided the backbone for the administration of a vast empire that was once the envy of the World. At Malvern we sometimes felt that parts of our education were ill thought out (certain aspects of the Combined Cadet Force, and mandatory boxing, for instance), but it was at Caterham that we learned the value of many of these lessons for which our parents had paid so much. On this particular day it was boxing that shone forth.

We were in the massive gymnasium on rope-climbing exercises, Guards fashion. Any errors in technique led to the order for all six recruits to climb their rope again, in-line formation. After a few mistakes had inspired several repeat attempts, the exercise became agonising, not to say frightening, as hands and forearms gave the feeling of failure, high above the floor.

One super-fit Physical Training Instructor (PTI) ran the exercise. His assistant would be responsible for the remainder of the squad, ensuring that there was no movement, or other gross idleness in the waiting ranks. On this occasion an Irish Guards squad was boxing nearby. One of our squad, Willie Pryor, submitted for an instant to temptation. He allowed his eyes, or even one of them, to wander in the direction of the Micks' boxing ring. As quick as a flash the piercing eye of our PTI, Lance-Corporal R. Painter, was on to him. "So, y'a wanna box, do you laddie?"
"Oh, no, Corporal," protested Willie.
"You wanna box, don't you?"
"No, no! Corporal!"
"Well, I think we can help you!" Turning to his senior colleague at the ropes the PTI yelled out, "Sergeant, we have someone here who wants to box the Micks."
"Oh! Do we indeed?" replied the PTI Sergeant, with a wicked smile spreading across his leather face. "Let's see if we can accommodate him. I feel sure we can."

After a brief discussion between PTI's and the Chief PTI the match was arranged. Indeed, it promised to be such a spectacle that, in what passed as a rare example of generosity, other squads were allowed to watch what promised to be a short, bloody but entertaining fight. Or was it just to 'witness punishment'? I say short because there were no weight limits. This was to be an 'open' challenge. The Mick PTI handpicked his biggest and best fighter to fight a 'pansy' potential officer. The Mick was a huge, well-muscled figure for whom the word 'grizzled' might have been invented. He looked as if he had seen the odd 'duff-up' in the rougher pubs of Dublin. Willie Pryor, on the other hand, looked pale and far smaller, almost undersized, with a jaw and nose so pointed that they presented inviting targets.

The Mick PTI addressed the excited company. "Right! Today, we have a challenger from the Brigade Squad. That's the squad of potential f****** h'officers, who think they're as tough as the Irish!" This announcement provoked a carnivorous roar from the assembled crowd.

"Come here, laddie. What's y'er f****** name, then?"
"Recruit Pryor, Corporal," stammered a shaking Willie.
"Recruit Pryor...the challenger!" yelled the PTI, to a roar of boos. "Get to y'er f****** corner!"

The atmosphere was electric, even by Caterham standards. Everyone sensed they were about to witness a massacre. Willie, dwarfed by his opponent, looked noticeably intimidated, yet he was as lean and fit as a greyhound. Moreover, he was about to fight for his life and poised for action.

The bell sounded and both boxers came forward to touch gloves. The Mick started to dance around the ring in a well practised manner, like a cat sizing up a cornered mouse, teasing out a chance to end it all with a single blow. Willie, on the other hand, just flew into a wild attack. As he later recounted, he was so scared that his only option was all-out frontal assault. He offered no defence. Every ounce of his thought and energy was put into the attack. He literally flew at his giant opponent, fists flailing - left, right, left, right, left, right, non-stop, and at about 200 paces to the minute - a Grenadier might have boxed in a more regimental manner (left, left, left, right left.) and at a more sedate 120 paces to the minute! Like everyone else, the Mick was stunned. He started to retreat. But Willie kept 'a cumin'. On and on he came, left and right. The Mick was now fully on the defensive, with apparently little defensive experience or skill. Willie landed some punishing blows. The Mick's rudimentary guard dropped and Willie seized his chance. The giant Mick fell to the floor in a deep sleep. There was uproar. Amidst the cheers and boos, the Mick was counted out. To his indignant disbelief, the Mick PTI raised the hand of our new hero, Willie, exhausted, nose bleeding, but smiling and with all his teeth. We were literally all 'chuffed to NAFFI breaks'. Trained Soldier Williams awarded us an extra half hour in the NAFFI that memorable night. Willie, unsurprisingly, was guest of honour.

This was not just a magnificent victory for Willie Pryor; it was a decisive victory for the whole Brigade Squad. Willie had been picked at random to face the Pride of the Irish. He had not only won. He had won in very short order and by a dramatic knockout. He was our hero and we all came in for some reflected glory. News of the contest spread like wildfire. As far as the recruits of our era at Caterham were concerned, every man was a hero in the Brigade Squad. All other recruits viewed us with respect in the mess hall and in the NAFFI. Never again did anyone look like he was even thinking of swiping food from our plates. We were all seen as heroes and dined both in and out on it!

Chapter 3

Posted Missing

*O*ur squad instructor, Sergeant Dunks and our Trained Soldier, Williams, were the epitome of toughness. However, both were fair, displayed their human side and, largely at our expense, had an excellent sense of humour. If they felt we had done well we were rewarded with small but valuable increments of freedom. The most important of these was the granting of strictly limited time to run to the NAFFI and back. Long queues on arrival at the NAFFI often forced us to return, breathless, and empty handed. (After deduction of stoppages, we were paid out one pound Sterling a week, so this was not all bad as it was a forced saving of cash).

One exception was the lucky recruit who that night earned the distinction of collecting the Trained Soldier's requirements. He had no time limit and was allowed to stay until served. Even then there was a downside - returning to our hut alone he provided an irresistible target to any ill-intended Trained Soldier that spotted him. Brigade Squad small fry were tasty! He was then 'rifted' in double time. If, as a result, he spilt too much of the Trained Soldier's tea it was back to the NAFFI for a refill, at his own expense.

Another favour to be earned was the right to bring back an electric gramophone after a rare Saturday evening out of barracks. I think it was Jamie Eykyn's father who smuggled in from New York a copy of the recording of *My Fair Lady*, yet to be released in England. The Broadway musical's show-stopping tunes raised our morale for nights on end. Subsequently they raised much more at deb dances.

In bitter early winter conditions our most important item of comfort, as so often in war, was warmth. We were responsible for heating our own water and living space, using ancient apparatus of First World War origin. This important task was appropriately assigned to the Household Cavalry, surely to be trusted to keep us all comfortable? In particular this responsibility fell to Recruit The Marquis of Dufferin and Ava (Blues) and Recruit The Lord Walpole (Life Guards). Walpole was later invalided out and replaced by Auberon Waugh (Blues, his father Evelyn's former regiment).

The Household cavalrymen ('Donkey Wollopers') proved to be experts at keeping us warm and comfy. After 'lights out' a reassuring glow from our red-hot stoves was visible. However, our two esteemed 'Donkey Wollopers' were not so hot on accounting. Coke stocks dwindled at an alarming rate and an emergency meeting was called in the showers. It was noted that a post and rail fence ran alongside our lines, surrounding a paddock used to keep the Military Chargers of the Commanding Officer, the Second-in-Command and the Adjutant. It was also noted that the parallel rails were modest wooden planks stapled onto plain, un-barbed, parallel wires. In short, they were not indispensable. Without them a presentable post and plain wire fence would remain, good enough to restrain horses, particularly as no semi-intelligent horse would wish to swap a grass field for the Guards depot! So a decision was made to use the parallel rails as our next source of fuel, to be taken down piecemeal, as required, after dark and briefly stored in the boiler hut (inspected infrequently, and then only in daylight).

A few weeks later we passed out and gave a dinner for our instructors. The Grenadiers included Colour Sergeant Nash (administration) and Sergeants Brown (weapon training), Sharman (alternate) and Dunks. Most of our squad then left for officer training school – the Household Cavalry to Mons and the Foot Guards to Eaton Hall. Those destined for Sandhurst, and those given a second chance at the War Office Selection Board stayed behind for a week or two, unsquadded. We were quartered in a barrack room with 5 Company, Irish Guards as 'fatigue fodder'. Our various duties included mounting the Marrath Stone in the barrack block gardens of 14 Company Grenadier Guards.

It must be said that although we had passed out of Caterham we had not been on the required 12 weeks of field training at Pirbright in Surrey, nor the fortnight of battle camp at Pickering, Yorkshire. We were therefore not considered to be fully Trained Soldiers. Being unsquadded, we felt more vulnerable. However, the boxing legend of Willie Pryor lived on and we were largely left alone. Additionally, we were allowed out on some evenings. To her credit, Sheridan Dufferin's mother, The Dowager Marchioness, continued to invite some of us to her sumptuous Knightsbridge home. Such entertainment provided a brief opportunity to re-charge our batteries with some high living.

Returning from one of these enviable excursions, our train stopped incessantly. After several hours had passed and long overdue at the Depot, We feared for our well-being. The convivial effect of fine wine was wearing off, big time. We were eventually told that there had been a collision on the line ahead. One of us (no names, no pack drill) remarked that he hoped the incident might be serious enough to make the headlines and so reduce our punishment. In the event, the crash at Hither Green, south London, was one of the worst ever recorded.

Finally we reported back at the Guards Depot gate. "You're five hours late! Not five minutes, but five f****** hours late!" cried the Sergeant of the Guard. "Put 'em in the cells. Ties off, boot laces out, braces off!" (no idle suicide precaution at Caterham). We spent the rest of the night in a cell, on a wooden board bed, with inlaid wooden pillow and one blanket, to reflect upon the morrow.

The next day we were marched in on Memoranda in front of Major Plumber, commanding 5 Company Irish Guards. The tragedy known as the Lewisham Train Disaster had claimed many lives. Our case was dismissed.

Some days later we were on fatigues near our old huts when the Adjutant (Captain Harrison, Scots Guards) came on a Round of the Barracks, accompanied by Sergeant Major Fred Clutton. All appeared to be going well, the Sergeant Major getting a 'grip' of any squad or person in sight, when the Adjutant decided to look at the stables. As he came out, his eyes gazed fondly at three contented horses grazing in the paddock, seemingly oblivious to the approach of an immense military presence. Then the Adjutant's eye fell on the post and rail fence, by now reduced to a post and wire fence. "Sergeant Major!" he called out.

"Sir!" replied Clutton, who was just concluding some strong words of 'advice' to the soldier groom at the stable door, on how to look "less 'orsy".
"Where the hell's the post and rail fence?"
Slowly, very, very slowly, lest we draw attention to ourselves, we slid behind out old hut; our first and last refuge at Caterham!

The Royal Military Academy
Sandhurst

Lessons learned at Caterham made the first term at Sandhurst a lot easier. Basic drills, administered superbly, mainly by Guards instructors, were much the same, but there was a welcome absence of fear so characteristic of Caterham. Notable Grenadiers I remember included: Major James Scott (Adjutant. Afterwards, Lieutenant-Colonel Sir James, Baronet. Later, Commanding Officer of the Life Guards, and Lord Lieutenant for Hampshire when I was MP for Winchester); Major Arthur Sparatley MBE, MM (Quartermaster. Subsequently a Lieutenant Colonel); and, the unforgettable J.C. Lord, MVO, MBE. John Lord, also known as 'Jackie', played rugby for the Army and represented his battalion at cricket and tennis. He earned a God-like reputation, following his capture as a parachutist after the Arnhiem drop, as prisoner 117294, at Stalag XIB. He established such high Grenadier standards at the camp that, by the time liberation came, the relieving Coldstream Guards, commanded by Major Ralph Cobbold, thought the camp had already been liberated. This view reflected the high morale and turnout at the camp. Returning to duty, Jackie Lord was appointed Academy Sergeant Major – a post created as a personal tribute to a truly great Grenadier. (I felt most honoured when he accepted an invitation to attend my wedding.)

Others remembered were Company Sergeant Major Robert Woodfield (subsequently MBE, and Company Sergeant Major of the Guards Parachute Company). He is now a Major overseeing archives at Regimental Headquarters. Also there was Sergeant Day. The Grenadier Officer Cadets whom I knew included Nick Redmayne, Sword of Honour winner (afterwards, The Honourable Sir Nicholas, Baronet); Oliver Lindsay (now, Colonel Oliver, CBE); John Festing; Lord Patrick Anson (later The Earl of Lichfield); Henry Hanning; Paul Cordle and the Honourable George Jeffreys. However, with no Grenadier instructors in my Company, there were relatively few printable Grenadier Grins stories from Sandhurst days.

At Sandhurst there was plenty of sport. Soccer trials preceded rugby trials and, when I scraped into the soccer XI, rugby took a back seat. In our last season, we were captained by an old school adversary from Shrewsbury, Anthony Cordle (Coldstream Guards). We had great fun, including a football tour of Germany, finishing up in Berlin, before the Wall was built. Memorably, we played in the forbidding 1936 Olympic stadium, where one wit from the Royal Scots shouted out, to the amusement of the crowd, that I had missed heading a ball because I had no chance to see it: my hair was too long! Back in England we found ourselves stepping out onto another historic turf, Iffley Road, Oxford, surrounded by the hallowed cinder track where Roger Bannister, paced by Chris Brasher and Chris Chataway, ran the world's first Four-Minute Mile, in May 1954, the sporting coup of the century.

The Summer months were much invigorated by trips to London for dances (all white tie in those days). Once our regulation passes were exhausted, it was time to put into practice the 'escape and evasion' techniques we had been taught, sometimes against the Academy police, with dogs. It was all fine training, although it was not considered as such if we were caught! In 1958, partly as an excuse to be allowed out, at least half-way to London, I joined the Guards Polo Club. I came under the wonderful teaching and charming spell of the celebrated Major General Claude Pert (formerly Probin's Horse and a 9-goal player for England's pre–war 39 goal side). To polo players, Claude Pert's voice was to the game much like match commentaries by Grenadier Major Brian Johnston MC and John Arlott - one of my future constituents - were to cricket lovers. At Windsor I started a life-long love affair with polo, providing me with much unimpaired happiness at Harvard and elsewhere, including Cyprus, France and Germany. Sadly, however, polo put cricket on the back burner, for I never played another serious game, other than for show as President of the Hursley Cricket Club.

While at Sandhurst, I was greatly privileged to be accepted as a private military history student by none other than Captain Sir Basil Liddell-Hart. Badly gassed in the First World War, he was one of our country's foremost military thinkers and historians. Indeed, he was perhaps the single most important designer of a method of conducting armoured warfare that his German students later christened Blitzkrieg. During the inter-war years he was also a very close confidant of Winston Churchill, Lawrence of Arabia, Bernard Montgomery and many key German generals, including Guderian (from whom he had a letter addressed to 'The Captain who teaches Generals'), Kesselring and Rommel. (I actually met Field Marshal Kesselring in 1950, when he was still a political prisoner of war. When I was in Germany with the Second Battalion in the early 1960's, I visited Kesselring at his home in Baden Baden, after his release from prison. He gave me a beautiful portrait of himself in the full dress uniform of a German Field Marshal. On the reverse side he wrote a brief dedication to me. It included the words, 'May youth be the bridge between the occidental peoples'). After an afternoon of tutorial at Liddell-Hart's house in Maidenhead, he would hold me spellbound, over dinner, with his stories of times and famous men of the past.

Just before leaving Sandhurst, Henry Hanning's father, Colonel Arthur Hanning OBE, (Grenadier Guards and Captain of Invalids at the Royal Hospital, Chelsea), invited me to the Oak Apple Day Parade. Her Majesty, The Queen Mother, took the salute. I understand that one Chelsea Pensioner on parade, but sitting in rear, was wearing the Kadive Star (1892). If true, it must have been a near record.

Royal Military Academy Sandhurst
6-a-side soccer cup winners, Marne Company
1958

R.M.A Sandhurst. Drill competition 1959, Marne Company
*At top, a 'decapitated' Major Gilbert Lamb, Grenadier Guards,
Inspecting Oficer*

Photograph by Marshalls of Camberley

Chapter 4

Nasty Rumors

Sandhurst, Spring 1958

The Junior Under Officer in charge of our junior platoon in Marne Company was Ronnie McCrum (destined for an outstanding career, I think, in the King's Own Scottish Borderers). He was a fine young man, much respected as a strict disciplinarian. Unfortunately, for him, his birthday fell when we were in his 'care'.

He had taught us so well that we hatched and executed a copybook kidnap plan. A little after midnight, with security slackened, we stormed his room, muffled and tied him up. We took him to the Seniors' car park and, in two smuggled-in motor cars, drove through the back gates towards a boathouse on the Thames, where we 'secured' two rowing boats, from a previously reconnoitred place. We rowed Ronnie to an island, some distance from the riverbank. We left him there, in his pajamas, but with loosened bindings, his greatcoat, a pair of boots, a bottle of whisky, one of the boats and, of course, a birthday card. We rowed away, returned our boat and beat it back to our rooms undetected.

Ronnie Mc Crum was absent from the Breakfast Roll Call (BRC) parade. There was some debate amongst his fellow senior cadets including our Cadet Sergeant, Ian Purvis-Hume (Argyll and Sutherland Highlanders), and our Senior Under Officer, Gerald Ward (Blues). A search of Ronnie's room revealed the mess caused by the evening escapade. We expressed consternation, but silent mirth.

Ronnie eventually shed his bindings and rowed ashore. On the long walk back to Sandhurst, carrying the whisky and birthday card, he spotted a milk float, which he hailed in the hope of a lift. The driver slowed down, but as he approached our Ronnie, dressed in army issue pajamas and khaki greatcoat, it occurred to him that this may just be an escaped inmate from the local lunatic asylum. The milkman suddenly accelerated away to report the incident. The next vehicle Ronnie flagged down was a police car. He was taken into custody and returned to Sandhurst for identification.

Ronnie Mc Crum took it all very well and there was no immediate retaliation. His senior fellow cadets, however, were not so benign. They soon pieced together some of the facts and the ringleaders spent considerable time on Extra Drills!

A few days later, some of us assembled at the foot of the famous Academy steps in front of Old College, awaiting a dose of Extra Drills. To our surprise, Academy Sergeant Major J. C. Lord came past, with a half smile on his face. Suddenly the considerable figure stopped and stooped (a movement somewhat unfamiliar to a Grenadier) to pick up something from the parade ground. "A shilling, by God!" he exclaimed, holding it up. "A King's shilling, perhaps?" Then, turning towards us, he growled, 'but I don't expect any of you young gentleman to start any nasty rumours that you saw the Academy Sergeant Major looking at the ground!" At this point, a few drops of rain fell. Our hearts rose at the chance that Extra Drill might take place inside, with less wide-open space for us to cover with our sweat. But, no such luck. Sergeant Major J. C. Lord looked skywards, towards the 'other' Lord JC, and departed shouting, "Keep them outside Sergeant Pittaway. It's only a little rain. I always say, 'the worse the weather, the better the drill!' Carry on, Sergeant." "Yes Sir!" responded Pittaway.

The showers left behind puddles not only filled with rainwater. Much of it was our sweat. We certainly paid more than petrol money for Ronnie Mc Crum's birthday arrest!

Chapter 5

Mid-Air Arrest

The only way to get rid of temptation, is to yield to it.
—Oscar Wilde

RAF Abingdon, Parachute School, Summer 1959

The parachuting section of the 'Edward Bear' parachute course at Sandhurst was conducted by the Parachute School, RAF Abingdon. There, highly competent instructors were charged with getting some senior cadets through the course without serious mishap. It was a challenge for any instructor. For cadets, standard punishment was a summary order of on-the-spot press-ups: 10, 20, or even 30, depending upon the degree of assessed idleness in the performance of the exercise. Examples would be an 'idle exit' from the aeroplane, lacking aggression, or leaving a 'twist-causing' leg hanging out behind one's body.

Most British-trained parachutists would probably agree that the worst jumps are the first two, from the static barrage balloon, a nerve-stretching 800 feet above ground. The wide-open hole in the floor of the gondola, swaying quietly beneath the balloon and the 200-foot vertical drop, with no slipstream to cushion the fall before the parachute opens, are both stomach-curdling experiences. Our bodies do not take naturally to parachuting, and it is definitely 'mind over matter'. It is this sense of personal achievement that helps greatly to increase the morale of airborne forces.

Our final daylight jump was an occasion for some celebration. Feeling something special was called for, I thought it might be timely for a wild fox hunting "hulloo" from our jumping sticks. I therefore carefully stowed my foxhunting horn (polished to a high Grenadier standard) inside the chest zipper of my parachute smock. It went undetected. The whole jump would last only a minute in the air, so I had to make a good exit to gain time for a few seconds of 'toot.'

Luckily, all went well with my jump: exit without 'twists' in the lift cords; parachute opening perfectly, without tears; no one in line for a mid-air tangle or collision; weapons container released on its retaining rope without incident; excellent sunlight and only a light wind over the dropping zone. I reached inside my smock for my hunting horn and sounded a brief 'gone away', before returning it, grabbing my lift webs and lining up for landing. The whole stick replied with loud "hollas."

I landed okay and was smiling as I gathered in my parachute. Without warning a Land Rover appeared. A Sergeant shouted out, "Was that you with that trumpet thing, Sir?"
"I sounded a hunting horn, Staff," I replied, beginning to feel a lot less gruntled.

"Sir, you're under Open Arrest. The Chief Instructor thought it was somebody in trouble and screaming. Now, *you're* in trouble. Get in the back with your chute." Once inside the Land Rover, the Sergeant looked at me over his shoulder in a concerned manner, adding. "I don't think you'll remain a Senior Under Officer for much longer, Sir." I was dropped at a hut by the side of the airfield and put through a strenuous régime of almost continuous press-ups during the refreshment break after the jump.

Looking at it now from a more relaxed viewpoint, the day went well and every one, including instructors, was in high spirits. I don't know what happened, or whether the Sergeant ever reminded the Chief Instructor that he held me in Open Arrest. I was finally driven back to barracks and heard nothing more and, amazingly, remained a Senior Under Officer until our Passing Out Parade. This was all thanks to something. Exactly who or what, I never discovered. I just wonder if it could have been Guards loyalty?

RAF Abingdon, Summer, 1959
JB in very 'open' arrest!

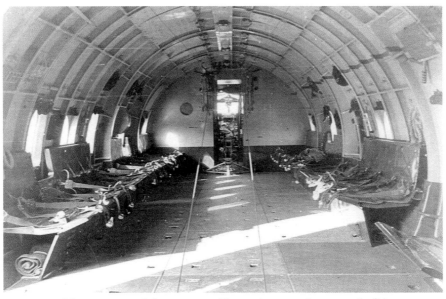

Noise terrible: even the stewardesses left!

2nd Bn Colour Party,
Germany
1961

No 2 Guard, 2nd Bn, Queen's Birthday Parade
(on grass) Düsseldorf, 1960

Part Three

Life in the Second Battalion

('The Models') 1960

It was a great privilege to return to the Grenadier Guards as a commissioned Officer and it was with a sense of anticipation that in the following year I was posted to the 2nd Battalion ('The Models'), stationed in Germany. The objective was to try and put into practice some of what we had learnt, with fine soldiers under command. However, my return to the Regiment did not go as smoothly as I had hoped!

Looking back, it was all very long ago, but it said much for the times that we were dressed and equipped in the same type of kit as worn by our Second World War predecessors: woollen battledress, studded ammunition boots and gaiters. We had only recently shed our.303 Lee Enfield Mark 4 Rifles for the 7.62 Self Loading Rifle and our web equipment was blancoed, with polished brass fittings. VHF (Very High Frequency) radios were only just entering service.

Even on field training, the Officers' Mess sported regimental silver and the Colours. It was a different age. For instance, when in Sennelager, for battalion infantry/tank field training with our cavalry regiments, we took our polo ponies, kept in tented stables adjoining our battalion tented camp. In barracks our training for war even extended to mounted sword drill parades, for officers junior to the Adjutant, in the magnificent former German army riding school in our (Llannelly) barracks. The Adjutant supervised proceedings. Lieutenant Nigel Corbally Stourton, aided by Hans, our local riding master, managed the horses. Sergeant Major Fred Clutton or Drill Sergeant Joe Randall 'ran' the young officers, in muted, uncharacteristic *pianissimo* voices. Such memories are reminiscent of tales of the Indian Raj, rather than of a mechanized army, facing Cold War hordes of the Soviet-led Warsaw Pact forces. It was all good stuff for a peacetime posting. It may not have been modern war but must have puzzled the heck out of Soviet intelligence.

Our primary duty was to be in constant readiness to defend a sector of the Western bank of the River Weisser, against lightning assault by the massively superior armoured forces of the Warsaw Pact. We also took our turn in providing guards for the night train travelling through the Russian Zone of Germany, to and from Hanover in the British Zone and the British Sector of Berlin.

Originally we were mechanized infantry, with one regiment of tanks in support of each infantry battalion. The 17th / 21st Lancers supported us before their departure for Hong Kong, and the Inniskillen Dragoon Guards acted as replacement.

At long last, after the effect of nuclear parity was finally acknowledged by NATO Governments, it was understood that armour was needed to offer any realistic defence against Soviet aggression. In 1961 we were issued with 'Pig' lightly armoured personnel carriers. One entire cavalry regiment was assigned to support each infantry battalion (in our case, the 10th Hussars). Combat Kit of the plain green Korean War variety, new webbing and VHF (C42 and A41) wireless sets were issued, representing the first major re-equipping of the army since the Second World War. We felt decidedly modern!

Chapter 6

Mistaken Identity

Second Battalion Grenadier Guards,
Hubbelrath, Germany, Winter 1960

I passed out of Sandhurst at the end of 1959, spending Christmas and New Year at home in Wiltshire. The holiday ended with a call from Regimental Headquarters instructing me to meet a New-Draft squad, at King's Cross station, on its way to join the 2nd Battalion in Germany.

I left Wiltshire with heavy luggage, and all my new uniforms, driving to London with a friend who had agreed to return my motor car to its home base. That night we attended a party in London. We left many hours later. Unfortunately, we could not find my automobile. It took us a few minutes of slightly inebriated head-scratching to conclude that the motor car was stolen with all, but all, my possessions inside. After a long walk to Chelsea police station and an even longer wait, the vehicle was found and returned less all my kit, except for a fox hunting horn and one best boot!

The following day was my baptism of fire as a Grenadier officer and it looked as if I would not make it to an overseas sailing parade. In a panic, I beat a hasty path to the old Reservist store at Wellington barracks. The Colour-Sergeant was at a loss until, eyeing me closely and holding his chin he said, "Well, Sir, you are shorter, but you do look about his body size. It may be worth a try."
"Whose size?" I asked in amazement.

"Well, Sir, we have the kit of an officer who has unfortunately been shot and killed. It may just fit you."

"What?" I blurted out.

"He was a fine officer, rest assured, Sir. His kit will all be in good order. We can do some minor alterations."

The dead Major's kit, duly unpacked, was tried on, item by item. It was a shade spooky but 'you don't look a gift horse in the mouth' particularly when you are at risk of missing a maiden posting overseas. As the Arabs say, "God was kind". The pairs of trousers were long, but almost everything else fitted. Even the hats were only slightly tight. A lone Garter star on each shoulder replaced the deceased Major's crowns. The uniforms were pressed and the brasses buffed. That was roughly how, in a matter of hours, I was on my way to King's Cross with very light baggage.

Within minutes of arrival a smart, former member of The King's Company put his feet impressively 'into' the platform and saluted crying out, "Sergeant Perkins, Sir. Reporting with the New Draft for the second battalion Sir!" Not only was I scruffier than usual, but this was also my first military engagement since the Sandhurst Passing Out parade and the Christmas holidays had been *very* good, but not at all military in outlook. I proposed a drink and Sergeant Perkins soon filled me in. A coffin bearer to King George VI, he was present in the King's Guard during the dismounting from Buckingham Palace, and blown flat by the German flying bomb that destroyed the Guards' chapel. His extended family led to the special entitlement of two married quarters. (A photograph in the 2004 *Grenadier Gazette* suggests Sergeant Major Lincoln Perkins may be one of his children.)

A particularly rough crossing from Harwich to the Hook of Holland was followed by an interminable train journey. Eventually, we arrived at Hubbelrath barracks. I found my way to the Officers' Mess and met Lieutenant Nigel Corbally Stourton, sitting with his feet up and looking at his most regimental in full riding kit. A keen horseman, and captain of the battalion polo team, he arranged a lot of our sporting activities, not least polo against our cavalry regiments, when on infantry/tank cooperation field exercises at Sennelager. It would be inaccurate to say that he welcomed me. (In those far off days, newly-joined officers were barely acknowledged for a week or so). Yet, having discovered 'what' rather than 'who' I was, he informed me there was a Dinner Night that evening, where I would be required to wear mess kit. On learning that I had none, not even a dinner jacket, he was generous enough to lend his own.

That night, I met most of my fellow officers. From memory these included: brevet Lieutenant-Colonel David Fraser (Senior Major, and later General Sir David, GCB, OBE, Vice Chief of the General Staff); Majors: Lionel Harrod (afterwards Major General Lionel); Michael Giles; Gavin Anderson; Christopher Airy (later, Major General Sir Christopher, KCVO, CBE); David Martin; Captains: Greville Tufnell (Adjutant, and later Colonel Greville, CVO, in charge of The Queen's Body Guard of the Yeoman of the Guard); Dermot Blundell-Hollinshead-Blundell (Signals Officer, later a Brigadier); James Alston-Roberts-West (Mortar platoon); Montague Cholmeley (later Sir Montague, Baronet); William Hopton-Scott (Assistant Adjutant); Lieutenants: Michael Healing (Motor Transport Officer); Timothy Barnes; Mark Dury; William Saunders; and Second Lieutenants: John Festing; Henry Hanning and Charles Blackwood.

The Quartermasters were two delightful senior Grenadiers, Arthur Everett and Sidney Felton. Most had served in the battalion during the Cyprus emergency and formed a tightly-knit group. In particular, Dermot Blundell, Jamie West, Nigel Corbally Stourton, Michael Healing and Monty Cholmeley executed some sensational high jinks. One was so spectacular that our Brigade Commander, Brigadier John Nelson (afterwards Major-General Sir John, KCVO, CB, DSO, OBE, MC) was compelled to dock Monty Cholmeley several months Captain's pay. He must have regretted such a decision when Monty elected to marry his delightful eldest daughter.

At dinner I sat next to the Commanding Officer, Lieutenant Colonel James Bowes-Lyon, cousin of The Queen, and squadron leader in the 2nd (tank) Battalion in the Second World War (afterwards, Major General Sir James, KCVO, CB, OBE, MC). He was a remarkable Edwardian man who 'sang' rather than 'spoke' English. He told me that he approved of young officers being out late at night provided they were fit for the next morning's parade: "it teaches them one of the most valuable lessons in war, which is dealing with a serious lack of sleep!"

In the morning I was 'seen' by the charming but rigorous Adjutant, Greville Tufnell, and later 'welcomed' officially by the Commanding Officer. Referring to my lack of full uniform and personal kit he declared, "you cannot go on living in a dead man's clothes". Turning towards the Adjutant he said, "he must be sent back to England so that he can get himself properly kitted out."

"Sir!" replied Greville Tufnell.

Then, turning his eyes back to me, said, "By the way, if you have any trouble paying for all this new kit, you can borrow the money from me and you can pay me back at any time you feel inclined." Standing behind him was our Senior Major, brevet Lieutenant Colonel David Fraser. He beamed approvingly. On all counts I thought Colonel James an incredibly fine gentleman, and on recounting my experience to other young officers, found that it was conduct typical of the man. Colonel James truly saw himself as the 'father' of the young officers under his command and they all worshipped him. (Fortunately, I graduated from Sandhurst with two scholarships – one from Malvern, and one from the Academy – and was therefore relieved of borrowing any money for the replacement uniforms).

I was posted to No 2 Company, under Major Gavin Anderson, the other company officers included Lieutenant Mark Dury, renowned for his unrivalled sense of humour, and later Second Lieutenant Anthony Fry. Ray Page was the Company Sergeant Major.

A few weeks later, playing scrum-half in our battalion rugby team in a BAOR tournament, I received a major blow above the left eye. I was carried off to the Medical Inspection Room (MI), where the local battalion doctor put in four stitches, without anesthetic, before expertly plastering me up with tape. Back in the match, I was moved to the 'safer' position of centre three-quarter, but was never fast enough to do any damage. It was just a case of having 15 men on the field and passing the ball as soon as I received it.

Following the match, the shock wore off and the pain increased. On our return to Lannelly barracks, Captain Ron Geddes, our battalion doctor, insisted on taking out the original stitches, replacing them with a further six, better 'sighted' ones. All in all, the left side of my face looked a right mess.

It took weeks to arrange a passage in those less hurried days of train and ship but I finally received instructions to return to London for some military shopping duty. Before departure Greville Tuffnell said, "Oh, by the way, I want you to take these two officers' swords back to Regimental Headquarters so that they can be repaired."

"Sir!" I replied enthusiastically, bucked up at the thought of the inviting nightlife back in Jolly Old England (fraternisation with Germans was still much frowned upon in those far-off days).

We travelled in uniform in that era. Carrying only a lightweight suitcase. I asked my Soldier Servant to strap the swords to the side. I was driven to Düsseldorf station in an Austin Champ. My last visit had been to bid farewell to the 17th / 21st Lancers. A beautifully conducted affair that was a joy to see. Reminiscent of the Raj, it occupied an entire platform and the best part of an hour. The Grenadiers provided the Officers' Mess; the Scots Guards ran the Sergeants' Mess and the Oxfordshire and Buckinghamshire Light Infantry a canteen for the men. The corps of drums of all three regiments played - to the astonished admiration of the German public. The 17th / 21st travelled as an entire regiment, including families, and drew into the main station in an extra long train. *En route* to Hong Kong, via England, it was an epic party. Some were literally carried back aboard the train.

As I dismounted from the Champ, I noticed people staring and pointing in my direction. In particular, a number of parents were pointing out my arrival to their children. Even the gate attendants, with a look of wide admiration, saluted me (by then, rare in a German official). It was several weeks since the Lancers' farewell and I could not see why I was a focus of such attention. One father gestured towards the two swords, and then towards my heavily stitched left eye. My hair was relatively short and, dressed in a blue-grey greatcoat with a blue, gold braided, service dress cap, I realized that I did look just a little like a Heidelberg duelling student, albeit in a dead man's clothes!

School of Infantry, Hythe, 1960
JB clearly disbelieving a 'gigantic' Coldstream
claim by Lt. Willie Rous
(Note: old web equipment with brass fittings
and sleeveless leather jerkins, introduced in
WWI and phased out in early 1960's)

Chapter 7

"Well, That's Field Medicine For You!"

Bad Toltz, Bavaria, Winter 1961

*Colonel James Bowes-Lyon, considering our battalion should be fit to fight in winter snow conditions, sent a company at a time for a week under canvas to a mountain top at Winterberg. Training was enlivened when attempts were made to teach us to ski. We were each issued with a pair of ex-*Wehrmacht *skis (mostly without steel edges) and two studs to hammer into the back of the heel of each ammunition boot to hold the bindings. We were all fit, and injuries were surprisingly few. Intense cold ensured that whisky went cloudy, and beer turned to ice the moment the pressure top was released, yet it was all the greatest fun. One party, comprising the chief participants in the Army Ski Championships, staying in the main Winterberg hotel, was truly a riotous affair. Indeed, The Riot Act was famously read out by a senior staff officer. It was the first and only time I have heard it read.*

By chance, I won our final cross-country ski race. Unfortunately, the thrill was short lived, for the following year our new Commanding Officer, Lieutenant Colonel Anthony Heywood (Adjutant of the 2nd tank Battalion in the Second World War and subsequently a Brigadier, CBE, LVO, MC) appointed me captain of our battalion ski team. I did not make it into the downhill section but, because of my victory the previous year, I was 'sentenced' to a spell with the cross-country team. The daily routine-training consisted of some 20 kilometres skiing in the morning with about 10 kilometres of style-training in the *afternoon. Unlike most cross-country skiers, I was no cross-country runner. My appointment as captain, therefore, accounted for a lot of physical agony. For instance, after the shooting section, at the 10-kilometre point of the Army Patrol Race, we had to climb the downhill slope at Winterberg. In parts, it was so steep that it became a convex slope. At times like that, I regretted my small victory of the previous winter!*

After a year or so in Germany, several officers joined the battalion, including Anthony Fry; Philip Wright (later, OBE and a Deputy Sergeant at Arms, policing the likes of me, in the House of Commons); the Honourable George Jeffreys; Christopher Morgan-Smith; Anthony Lort-Phillips; Sam Weaver; David Hargreaves; Edward Aubrey-Fletcher; the Honourable David Brassey (now, The Lord Brassey); David Davenport (Transport Officer); and the Honourable Jeremy Monson. We also had a highly engaging American Exchange Officer, Captain William Tombaugh. He was, as the saying has it, very 'good news'.

*I*n 1961, the site chosen for our ski training and for battalion skiing was the Bad Toltz American army base in Bavaria, next to the Braunak Mountain. The barracks were warm, well-built and beautifully situated, with good American food. They were much enjoyed by all. Our ski team trained there for about six weeks, while each company rotated. There was certainly no more enjoyable period than when Captain, Jeremy Monson, his charming and beautiful wife Tisha, and Captain Tim Barnes were passing through.

One sunny day, after finishing our 20-kilometre morning training bash, with Sergeant Jewel and our team, our instructor took us over to the nursery slopes where one of the rifle companies was under instruction from Sergeant Saville's downhill team. Unfortunately, one novice guardsmen sat back on his skis. Out of control, and frozen with apprehension, he tobogganed on the back of his skis down the slope at ever-increasing speed, heading straight for a barn, mounted on stilts at the bottom of the sloping field. His skis and knees went underneath, and his first points of contact with the barn were his face and chest. He fell back, unconscious. We all skied down to help. The doctor, Captain Ron Geddes, RAMC, who, with George Jeffreys, was in our downhill team helping to coach the men, skied to a smart 'christie' halt, in a flurry of snow.

We crowded round to watch the marvels of modern medicine performed in the revival of the poor guardsman. The doctor got out of his skis to tend the fallen figure who, somewhat winded, regained consciousness. After he came round, the doctor examined his face, neck, arms and legs. All of us thought he would produce something dramatic out of his magical medical bag. He stood up and stepped back. We expected some learned diagnosis and a request for assistance. Instead, he merely said, "Okay, Get up and walk."

We were stunned, until a wag from the back row called out, "Well, that's field medicine for you!" We all, including our casualty who was being assisted to his feet, collapsed in laughter. It *was* field medicine—no malingerers in the Grenadiers!

School of Infantry, Hythe, 1960
Lindsey Stemp (Northumberland Fussiliers, skeptical of offer of Coldstream tea by Richard Macfarland

Second Battalion, Grenadier Guards,
Hubbelrath, Germany, 1961
Commanding Officer (Lt-Col. A. Heywood) briefs
The Colonel (Maj-Gen. Sir Allan Adair Bt.) on
Reconnaissance Platoon equipment. Platoon
Commander, Lt. Martin Lockhart Smith,
in attendance

Chapter 8

Sailing, Sailing

Kiel, Germany. Summer 1961

Before leaving Germany, several additional officers joined from the former 3rd Battalion, upon its going into 'suspended animation', in the shape of the Inkerman Company. These included: Richard Corkran (Signals Officer and later, Lieutenant-Colonel, OBE). He was given the challenging task of training-me-up on matters signal, (62 and 19 sets with the old fashioned 'netting calls') and, specifically, Morse code, in preparation for the Regimental Signals Officer course at Hythe. Early morning Morse practice started at 0700 hrs at Hythe, until one passed out at 16 words-a-minute. Talk about not speaking at breakfast! A real incentive existed to gain an extra hour of kip, particularly on Mondays, following heavy weekends in the West Country! Richard Corkran was ably assisted by Colour Sergeant Ernie Mitchell; by Lance-Sergeants' Bob Jenkins and Colin Bishop; and by Lance-Corporal Gerry Chamberlain. I remain most grateful to these patient tutors.

Also posted to us were: Guy Ellerington (former Guards Parachute Company); John Agate; Henry Askew; John Dance; Peter Cartwright; Martin Lockhart Smith and Edward Barry (now, Sir Edward, Baronet). The last two included me in their roulette syndicate to do battle in the Baden-Baden's casino. We had some great fun with initial successes and much excitement. However, like members of most syndicates of that nature, we finally learned the painful lesson that, as in golf, amateurs seldom triumph over the professionals in the long-term.

weekend sailor, I volunteered for the 4th Guards Brigade Baltic Passage Races. We were allowed to use the Army Yacht Club fleet of four-berth sailing boats, built by the Germans between the wars to train young naval officers, and commandeered by the British in 1945. They were well-built, handy and comfortable craft with four on board. The 2nd Battalion entered two boats: I crewed on the first, captained by our new Commanding Officer, Lieutenant Colonel Tony Heywood. The skipper of our second boat was the Senior Subaltern, John Festing, eldest son of the Field Marshal.

Colonel Tony was an accomplished sailor. On the first leg to a fishing village in Denmark, our two boats tied for first place with a pair entered by Brigade Headquarters. Their lead boat was skippered by Brigadier John Nelson (Grenadier Guards). He was a most gallant patrolling ace in the 5th Battalion during the Italian campaign, who went on to command the 1st (Guards) Parachute Battalion, before London District, and subsequently the British Forces in Berlin. We all enjoyed an excellent dinner ashore in a typical fishing village. On the second leg, we tied again with Brigade Headquarters. The final, third, day promised to be a knife-edge affair. All was anticipation.

Jockeying for position around the start line, Colonel Tony asked if I could see John Festing's boat. I could not. He grabbed the binoculars from me to survey the fleet for himself. Tension grew as he also failed to sight our second boat. The five-minute gun sounded, so we had to get down to our start routine in earnest. We made a promising start and., after trimming our boat, I was ordered to search again for Festing's boat. I searched in vain. Colonel Tony handed me the tiller and searched a second time himself, exhaustively. Still, no second boat came into view. This routine was repeated several times during the day, until our second boat was finally sighted, far in the rear.

For a third day running, locked in a hard fight against Brigadier John Nelson's boat, the excitement of the race gave way to increased concern every time we looked back towards our second boat, now at last gaining on the stragglers. We closed towards Kiel harbour, in a neck-and-neck 'luffing' duel with the Brigadier's boat. Sometimes we were so close we could sense the strain on his crew's faces, camouflaged by smiles, of course!

Then, the Brigadier's boat unexpectedly appeared to judder, falling fast behind us. She had run aground with the Brigadier at the helm! We were all relieved not to be his navigator, or even the most junior member of his crew. There were more than a few expletives floating on the breeze. We all smiled, but our gloating was short-lived. In a few moments we crossed the finish line in first position, but our second boat was far behind. Other crews congratulated us as they finished, but we were concentrating on the position of our second boat. Colonel Tony was in a state of barely controlled exasperation.

Crossing the finish line, a deeply crestfallen and shamefaced John Festing tied up along side our boat. Evidently, he had allowed two of his crew to go shopping for supplies, but had forgotten to give them a time for their return. The wait, and late start, had cost us the race, but we did manage second, despite the mishap.

Poor John and poor Colonel Tony. I have only seen such rage surpassed once: by Lieutenant Colonel David Scott-Barrett, the Scots Guards Commandant of the Guards Depot at Pirbright. Early one morning, the immaculately smart, but on this occasion, unfortunate Lieutenant Julian Pope (Coldstream Guards, and Sandhurst compatriot) was a fraction overdue for his own platoon parade, before leaving for field exercises at New Zealand Farm. His dear wife drove him to the parade. He got out of his motor car to find that not only were his platoon sergeant and all his men waiting, but also the Commandant, resplendent in highly polished field boots and breeches, with a face like thunder. When aroused, Colonel Scott-Barrett proved the most fearsome of men. On this occasion, he was not just angry; he was apoplectic. He took off his smartly diced Scots Guards service dress hat, threw it down and stamped it flat in sheer disbelief that any Officer could possibly be late for his own parade. I had the feeling that Colonel Tony was in one such mood, but no Grenadier hat was to hand, so he held his cool, as they might say today!

Second Battalion Grenadier Guards
Drum Major Meyhew with Corps of Drums
Beating Retreat, Düsseldorf, 1960

Chapter 9

Grenadier Strippers?

"The trouble with resisting temptation is that it may never come your way again."   —*Korman's Law*

Hubbelrath, Germany, Autumn 1961

A grand farewell dinner-dance in the Officers' Mess was arranged before our departure from Germany. The Great and the Good were invited from various headquarters and missions from all over BAOR. The theme was French, with waiters dressed in berets and hooped rugby shirts and schooled in a few elementary words of the language. It was not without interest that Brigadier John Nelson, entering into the spirit of the evening, sowed utter confusion when he replied, giving his order in French. The highest praise was reserved for Philip Wright, who painted one of the cellars to create a continental night club setting. (Such a transformation, if completed months beforehand, would have been hugely popular, and boosted mess funds considerably.) The pinnacle of the evening's entertainment was a French-style cabaret, featuring a troop of strippers from a nearby Düsseldorf night club. The Signal Platoon floodlight operators were falling over themselves to volunteer for duties that night!

To the sound of soft, sensual music (like the Coldstream quick march played slowly!) performed by the Regimental Orchestra under the legendary Major Rodney Bashford, OBE, some nubile girls came onto the floor to dance in an all-but naked state, save for a small, lighted candle held in each hand.

As expected, they were met by stunned silence. Unexpectedly however, no laughter followed. Instead, a state of 'official' disapproval permeated the entire hall. Some senior Generals' eyes came out like organ stops, but they were met with ice-like glares from their equally senior wives who were very, very British. One could be forgiven for thinking that they were of the 'No sex please, we're British' variety. Their dagger-like glares froze any man who even looked like he may smile, let alone applaud. It was all rather embarrassing.

The tension mounted as the girls danced on without any acknowledgement. Then, the cavalry, or even better, the Household Cavalry, came 'gallopin' to the rescue over this seemingly unscalable social hill. Captain Christopher Wordsworth (Life Guards, 4th Guards Brigade headquarters, if my memory serves) rose gallantly to his feet and holding his glass aloft in a richly comical toast in honour of the dancing girls, called out, "Dashed good of these Grenadier wives to put on such a superb show!" The place collapsed in laughter and goodwill. Our name was saved.

"DASHED GOOD OF THESE GRENADIER WIVES TO PUT ON SUCH A SUPERB SHOW!"

50

Chapter 10

State Opening of Parliment
Central Point

In late 1961, the 2nd Battalion returned to London for a tour of Pubic Duties. We were based at Caterham Barracks, recently vacated by the Guards Depot. Whilst in London, I had the privilege of doing my first Queen's Guard with The Commanding Officer, Lieutenant-Colonel Anthony Heywood, as The Captain: with Captain David Davenport, as the Buckingham Palace Guard Commander and Sergeant Major Fred Clutton MBE, MM, the Warrant Officer. Soon afterwards, we had a new Commanding Officer, Lieutenant Colonel Francis Jefferson - Signals Officer of the 2nd (tank) Battalion in World War Two. We also had a new adjutant, Captain John Magnay. Fred Clutton was promoted to Quatermaster/Transport Officer and replaced by Sergeant Major Dennis Randall. ('Joe' Randall, who I understand lives in Cornwall, had a son in The Regiment. He also has a grandson, now serving as a Captain in The Regiment and set upon a very fine career.)

Additional officers joining the battalion included: the Honourable Peter Dixon (now Lord Glentoran. Olympic bobsleigh Gold Medal winner); Miles Lambert (formerly, Guards Parachute Company); Lindsay Morehead; Sandy Gray; Sam Weaver MBE; Lou Drouet MBE; Paul Cordle; Charles Acland; Richard Proes; Peter Thwaites; Arland Usher; George Rochfort-Rae; and John Smiley (subsequently, Lieutenant Colonel Sir John, Baronet). We also had an outstanding new Pay Master, Major Desmond Evans.

Once at Caterham, we had several new intakes of young officers including Hamish Gray-Cheape (afterwards Her Majesty's High Sheriff and now one of Her Majesty's Deputy Lords Lieutenant for Worcestershire); Michael Johnstone; Peter Bywater; John O' Connell (now Colonel John); Nicholas Thorne; Anthony Mather; Nicholas Boggis-Rolfe; Anthony Dennison-Smith (Subsequently, Lieutenant General Sir Anthony, KBE); The Master of Rollo (now, The Lord Rollo); James Pugh; Michael Westmacot; Nicholas Thorne and Algernon Heber-Percy (currently Her Majesty's Lord Lieutenant for Shropshire). Subsequently, on returning from British Guiana, some additional young officers joined the battalion, including Edmund Hudson (now Colonel Edmund, CBE) and Hubert de Lisle.

Based at Caterham, we used Wellington Barracks as a forming up point for Public Duties. For much of that time, Wellington was occupied by the Mounted Squadron of the Household Cavalry while their new Kinghtsbridge Barracks was being built.

*I*n the early 1960's, the Second Battalion, Grenadier Guards spent time field training at Thetford. Whilst there, I remember hearing a wonderful *Today* programme in which my Sandhurst compatriot, Lieutenant John Ridgeway (The Parachute Regiment), was greeted ashore after his epic row across the Atlantic with his Sergeant (Chay Blythe) by the broadcaster Jack de Manio.

On the eve of the State Opening of Parliament we returned by train to London. We were to provide street liners in the Mall, but with no time for reconnaissance of the ground. It was an honour to command the Colour Party, with Second Lieutenant Philip Wright carrying the Regimental Colour. It was the same Colour Party, including Sergeants Saville and Day, which we had fielded for some parades before we left Germany.

On the day itself, we paraded at Wellington Barracks. The formidable Sergeant Major 'Joe' Randall (subsequently MBE), gave us a final briefing as we formed up outside the old Officers' mess. (It was in this same mess that I was first presented to HM The Queen. Like many others, I was spellbound by her radiance. In 1947, I was glued to my wireless set listening to her 21st Birthday speach, from HMS Vanguard, off South Africa) I remember asking 'Joe' Randall just how we would know exactly *where* we were to take up our position in the Mall. He looked to the immaculate Drill Sergeant Ray 'Flash' Huggins, who was in attendance. "Drill Sergeant, you marked out the exact position, earlier this morning, did you not?"

"Sir!" replied Huggins, exuding enthusiasm, confidence and efficiency, all wrapped up in an ultra smart Grenadier full dress uniform. "I measured it out by pace stick and marked the Central Point with a large 'C' and a large 'P', with chalk, on a curbstone of the pavement of the Mall on the way to Admiralty Arch, Sir."

"So there you have it, Sir. Keep your eyes skinned for 'C and P' on the pavement. You can't go wrong, Sir." His last observation made me just a little worried. I had heard similar remarks before. They often represented an open invitation to disaster.

Several minutes later, I was marching the Colour Party down the Mall. My bearskin cap was a good one, with a classic regimental fringe of thick hair over my eyes. Peering through it, past the gently flapping Queen's Colour and on past my raised right arm, made it more than a little difficult to see detail on the passing pavement. Despite the fact that the police had the public standing a couple of feet back from the curbstones, I saw nothing like a chalk-mark.

After a while I became increasingly aware that the Admiralty Arch was looming ever larger to my front, and got the sickening feeling that we must have passed the Central Point. My concern mounted and was confirmed when Sergeant Day said, "Sir, I think we must have missed the Central Point as we are now way down the Mall." Being lost with a Colour Party either in war or on a State Occasion is never a good situation (with not even a compass or a map!). I thought it would be made worse if we turned around and were still unable to find the Central Point. Our predicament of being 'lost on parade', risked becoming not only a new form of charge, under Military Law, but also obvious to the public, who would rightly view it as farce. I thought it best to stop and wait for navigational 'help'. I therefore ordered the Colour Party to halt, order arms and stand at ease. We waited. However, my concern rose further when I looked surreptitiously around to find that, with my eyes fixed on the curbstones, we had entered the street lining ground, if memory serves, of the Scots Guards. Naturally, they were somewhat surprised to see us!

A few moments later, two senior officers approached on horseback. One was a Commanding Officer, the other his Adjutant. As I was holding the Queen's Colour they both had to salute it sedately with their swords. Having done so, the Colonel shouted a most imperious admonishment at me, "What the bloody hell do you think you're doing in my battalion area?" I felt he was about to say more, perhaps much more, when I noticed his horse begin to move backwards, with ears flattened. I do not know that much about horses, but this horse looked decidedly upset by the hostile shouting and appeared to be thinking of rising up on his hindquarters. I can't claim that the horse sympathised with me, but his movements unsettled the Colonel who, slumped forward, was clearly trained to ride only in forward gear. Furthermore, the Adjutant's horse, not wanting to be left alone, was also becoming more than a little excited. I felt that Winston Churchill's observation that, 'Horses are dangerous at both ends and most uncomfortable in the middle', was about to be proved horribly true. Correctly sensing trouble, the Colonel hastily cut short his discourse and rapidly barked out, "Get back where you belong!" He followed this with a hasty and perfunctory sword salute (far less stately than his first) and rode off whence he had come. The encounter appeared to amuse some of the crowd. Clearly they did not quite understand why two very senior mounted officers would salute a junior before delivering a severe admonishment. Some in the crowd were more aware and muttered about the Colours. I have to say that, despite my serious predicament, even I found it quite amusing.

Rather than be seen marching up and down the Mall, looking clearly lost, with the Colour Party and, to yet further public amusement, I decided to 'hurry slowly' in moving off. However, I kept a weather eye open on the two Scots Guards officers. Unfortunately, the Adjutant looked round. He then spoke to the Colonel who also looked round. Noting a certain amount of inaction on my part, they turned their horses around. They started to approach me again, but this time at a sitting trot, a highly dangerous pace for a Foot Guards officer! I could sense serious trouble brewing. I was in despair when, clearly sensing trouble and typical of all great Warrant Officers in the Guards Division, up strode Sergeant Major 'Joe' Randall,.He also was in a high state of agitation. I explained the situation to him, as I saw it. With him in attendance, we returned up the Mall, back towards Buckingham Palace and safe 'Grenadier country'.

After we had marched 100 yards or so, we noticed Drill Sergeant Huggins standing on the pavement. As we approached, he called out, "Here it is, Sir!" With his pace stick, he pointed down to the two letters 'C' and 'P', each boldly written in chalk on the curbstone, at his feet. "The only problem was, Sir, that this policeman (standing embarrassed, but smiling to one side and looking up at the sky) was standing on them, with one foot on 'C' and the other on 'P'!"

'MASTER'

10th Duke of Beaufort
(Blues)
MFH and
Master of the Horse
1976

Major Gerald Gundry
(16/5 Lancers) MFH
talking to
Anne Darling, wife of
Maj-Gen Douglas
Darling
(Rifle Brigade)
1976

Photographs by S. Hurwitz

Chapter 11

"No Good For Hunting Now Sir; Just Weddings"

Yet think not, huntsman, I rejoice
To see the end so near;
Nor think the sound of horn or hound
To me a sound of fear
*   —The Fox's Prophecy, 1871, —Anon*

Melton Mowbray, Winter 1962

One of the many privileges we enjoyed in The Regiment in those far off days was 'Hunting Leave'. It was up to three weeks a year and had to be used exclusively for fox hunting. The army had long believed that fox hunting was an excellent way to teach young officers how to 'read' ground. I believe that they were quite correct. Choosing one's own 'line' across unfamiliar country is an excellent and enjoyable way to learn this most valuable of skills. It is a skill that can and has saved the lives of many soldiers in war. At Melton Mowbray, where some people still hunted three horses a day, the fact that one had to 'nurse' a single army charger and keep up all day over the same high-fenced country also encouraged a further valuable lesson: the conservation of energy, so crucially important when deploying 'foot slogging' and heavily equipped infantry in the field of battle. For example, a longer 'line', but one free of plough, may prove to be far more energy efficient than a shorter one. It is perhaps interesting here to note the pivotal damage done to the French army at the Battle of Agincourt (when King Henry V won the throne of France) by French mud, not by English long bows, as old-fashioned history had patriotically but wrongly taught us! How history might have *been changed had the French commanders hunted foxes instead of women?*

I had been lucky enough to gain places both on the Winter Warfare course in Norway and on the prized Long Equitation course at Melton Mowbray. Unfortunately, I had also recently been appointed as Battalion Signals Officer. Our new Commanding Officer, Lieutenant Colonel Francis ('Fanny') Jefferson, considered that signals were vital and needed constant practice and attention. He therefore denied me the long absences required of both these courses. I handed the vacancies to my friend Lieutenant Phillip Wright. Luckily, our adjutant, Captain John Magnay, was not only a former Signals Officer, but also a keen foxhunting man. He had a certain sympathy for my loss of the Long Equitation course. He therefore agreed to my application for three weeks hunting leave.

The Household Brigade Saddle Club, based at Melton Mowbray, was used as the 'boarding school' of rest and recuperation for many of the army chargers used on State Occasions in the London Summer Season. Any officers on hunting leave were accommodated in the Royal Army Vetenary Corps headquarters mess at Melton.

Coming from the Somerset-Wiltshire boarder, we all had the greatest admiration for our local, adjacent 'shire' hunt - the Duke of Beaufort's 'Blue and Buff'. The legendary 'Master' (10th Duke of Beaufort) of the 'Blues', hunted the bitch pack. The formidable Major Gerald Gundry (16th / 5th Lancers), hunted the dog pack. (Gerald Gundry was a 'Surtees' type of character. To me, he looked like a wonderful, half starved deerhound. He died at 12.45 pm on Thursday 20th December 1990. The Beaufort Hounds did not find another fox until two days later, at 12.45 pm, on the Saturday. After a long and extraordinary double circle run, under Captain Ian Farquhar (12th Lancers), they killed this fox on Gerald Gundry's front door step. Do you feel goose pimples? I do.) The Beaufort Field Master was David Somerset (Coldstream Guards), now the 11th Duke of Beaufort.

Even relative to the 'Blue and Buff', the three main Meltonian hunts (Quorn, Cottesmore and Belvoir) were in the top class as far as both the quality of horseflesh and general standards of turnout were concerned. Red (often referred to wrongly as, 'pink' after the famous Meltonian tailor, Mr. Pink.) swallowtail coats and champagne topped boots were the order of the day. Top hats were worn, even with grey coats ("d'ye ken John Peel in his coat so grey") and had to look immaculate, at least at the Meet.

The pick of Army chargers were given to serving officers and men, with first choice going to those on leave from overseas postings. I was at Melton and hunting in midweek. Sometimes, I was given an excellent mount. On one occasion, I was allotted one of the best horses in the stable. He was called 'Brutus'. Apart from one maddening habit of rolling in mud, he was a good looking, courageous and honest jumping hunter. It was a great thrill to have such a fine mount in the historic 'Mecca' of English fox hunting since the eighteenth century.

'Brutus' carried me so well one beautiful day that we were up amongst the leaders, even of a quality Meltonian field. It was a great feeling as we cleared some challenging fences. 'Brutus' was a hero and, like a true war-horse, loved every moment of life at the 'front'.

I was just behind the Field Master and saw the large fox turn hard right, through a hedge and set out boldly across a big grass field, followed by the hounds. Curiously enough, neither the Huntsman nor the Whips followed the pack but went straight onto a road. They jumped into the road and galloped up the grass 'ride' along the roadside. I was slightly puzzled by this. Thinking I could conserve a little of 'Brutus' generous energy, I pulled back and turned right-handed to jump the hedge. This was a risk in unfamiliar country. However, it was a clear sunny day, with excellent going. The pace was very hot and there was no danger in sight. It was a very bad decision. Quite how foolhardy it was, I did not realize as I approached the hedge. But once in mid air I saw clearly, and with utter horror realized instantly just why the locals had gone straight on. There was a stout barbed wire fence on the far side of the hedge. We hit the top strand so hard it burst, luckily doing very little damage to dear 'Brutus'. But we took a major fall. I awoke, with a bleeding nose, in the arms of some farmers who had been watching on foot. Holding 'Brutus' one assured me that, although slightly scratched, he was unharmed. Another, bringing me my crushed top hat, remarked, "Tis no good for fox huntin' now, Sir, jus' weddin's!"

Footnotes:

1. In later years this silk hat was good enough to serve the Regiment, earning a major award in the form of disability compensation for three Grenadiers, making it possibly the highest earning top hat ever produced by Mr. Lock!

2. It was a great sadness, in 2004, to witness the possible end of traditional foxhunting in England for reasons not of cruelty, but of 'social engineering'. By giving 'Government time' to a backbench Bill and usurping the (dubious) Parliament Act to bypass the House of Lords, the Government effectively cheated our Constitution and Parliamentary Custom to force the Bill through. If effective, such a ban would, I feel certain, do subtle, but untold damage to our wonderful countryside in coming years. With such strong feelings, I flew over to London for all the big demonstration marches, including the demonstration in Parliament Square in September 2004. It was the first time that I had actually seen open hostility in the eyes of the British police. This was a great shock to me. I understand that they were specially selected. They certainly behaved in a manner quite alien to those who hitherto regarded our police force as neutral, clubbing the heads of law-abiding citizens in a manner that, if it were a Coal Miners' demonstration, would have resulted in an emergency Censure debate in the House of Commons. Several demonstrators were arrested, as were those who entered the floor of the House. (The latter were, of course arrested, quite correctly.) On my way back from the demo I called in for some refreshment at the Turf Club. There, I met the Secretary, Lieutenant-Colonel Oliver Breakwell MBE (Coldstream Guards), dressed in black tie. He said, "Hullo, John, what brings you over here this time, the Demo?"

"Yes, I've been there most of the day and just dropped in for a drink."

"Why aren't you coming to the Golf dinner tonight?"

"Oh, I would have loved to have done so, but I forgot it was tonight."

"Well you can still come, if you wish."

"What? I thought it was always oversubscribed?"

"Normally, it is. But tonight, we have some of our members in jail, from the demo!"

"But I haven't got a black tie with me."

"Oh, that's alright; we'll lend you one."

I enjoyed a fine golf dinner, possibly at the expense of one of our 'jail birds' of whose actions I strongly approved. I therefore felt I should do something for them and wrote them a note saying how proud their grandfathers (of whom I had known two), would have been of them. Then I bought a bottle of Turf Club champagne, hailed a taxicab and set off for to find them.

On arrival at King's Cross police station, I found the 'birds' had been moved. The police were concerned that some of the demonstrators would follow their heroes to picket their jail, so they kept moving them. After a very expensive pursuit by taxi around London's police stations, I ran them to ground. However, I was not allowed to see them. Instead their supervising officer came out to see me. She was a good-looking, no-nonsense police woman (of the type one used to watch in old British comedy films, such as the 'Carry' On series). Clearly, the police were not going to risk any charges of alleged police brutality! She told me firmly, but politely, "Mr. Browne, I will give the prisoners your hand-written note, but I cannot give them the champagne."

"Why not?"

"Because they have to testify!"

"Can't you open the bottle, give them a just a wee plastic cup each and share the rest around the police officers?"

"Mr. Browne, we're on duty! Of course we can't do any such thing. I 'm afraid you'll have to leave now, with your bottle." (Well done, I thought, at least some good old English police integrity!)

I returned, crestfallen, but with an elated taxi driver, to leave the bottle, at the Turf Club for collection by the 'birds'. The next day I left for America. However, I heard later that the bottle had been collected!

In my view, the ban – described by Roger Scruton as "a piece of vindictive legislation" – is an unjust restriction on the freedom of a minority. I agree with the late Gerald Gundry when he said he believed that no law will prove to be enforceable and that foxhunting will eventually be strangled only by urbanization.

" WHAT THE BLOODY HELL DO YOU THINK YOU'RE DOING IN MY BATTALION AREA ? "

Chapter 12

"Old Spice"

Caterham barracks, Spring Drills, 1962

During 'Spring Drills' it was customary for all young officers, junior to the Adjutant, to be formed into a squad and given quite a 'chasing' by either the Sergeant Major or by one of the two Drill Sergeants. It was very good for the men to see the cobwebs sweated off the young officers.

One sunny Spring morning at Caterham, Sergeant Major 'Joe' Randall was chasing the young officers' squad under the approving eye of the Adjutant, Captain John Magnay. Sweat was flowing freely, when suddenly 'Joe' Randall cried out, "Squad-halt!" Slowly and purposefully, he approached the panting squad. "Well what have we here? A strange smell; a very strange smell indeed." He continued to walk slowly and menacingly, up and down the gasping ranks, past a red-faced Hamish Gray-Cheape, a panting Algy Heber-Percy, a supremely fit, but clearly flushed John O'Connell and up to a sweating Philip Wright, sniffing loudly all the while. He then moved on past a snorting Nicholas ('MIT') Boggis-Rolfe. a white-faced looking Michael Westmacott, a decidedly flushed Anthony Dennison-Smith, (trying vainly, like a budding General, to breath 'regimentally' though his nose), up to a sagging John Browne (the last three had been dancing in the Garrison Club in London until about 3.00 a.m. that morning), sniffing loudly and repeating, "Where's it coming from?" Then he followed his nose towards the taller officers, passing a haggard-looking James Pugh, until he stopped beside a panting and sweaty Master of Rollo, exclaiming, "Here it is! What on earth is this, Sir?"

"Old Spice, Sergeant... Major," gasped David Rollo (the measured pause between the two last words causing even more rage).

"Old Spice! Good God Almighty. Old Spice! What on earth are young officers in the Regiment coming to these days?" He roared as he continued to pace about the squad. "Old Spice. Good God! In my day, young officers smelt of Guardsmen's sweat, beer and onions! Old Spice indeed. I hope to God the Russians don't find out, or they'll attack tomorrow!" Then, getting back to business, as the Adjutant smiled and turned away, he barked out, " I'll give you Old Spice... Squad...at the double...mark-time-le-ri-le-ri-le-ri-le-forward-marktime-forward-marktime-forward-le-ri-le-ri-le-ri-le! etc, etc, etc" We continued to sweat, needing not *old* spice, but *new* spice!

"WHAT THE HELL ARE YOU DOING HERE ?"
"ARE YOU A FUSILIER ?"
"NO, I'M A GRENADIER"

Escape from the Tower of London

"You will do foolish things, but do them with enthusiasm."
—Anon

HM Tower of London, January 1963

The Tower of London used to contain a Guards barracks. In the early twentieth century the Royal Fusiliers were given the barracks as their Regimental depot. The Foot Guards Officer of the Guard was allocated a permanent flat, or apartment in the Officers' Mess of the Royal Fusiliers. The Guard itself was housed in a temporary wooden hut between the Ravens Cage and the Bloody Tower—all very spooky. The Tower Guard paraded with the main body of the Queen's Guard, at Wellington Barracks and then travelled, by coach to the Tower, where a local Guard Mounting parade took place on the lawn in front of the Queen's House, the official residence of the Deputy Governor (In our day, this was Colonel Sir Thomas Butler Baronet, Grenadier Guards).

One raw Winter's day, I took over the Tower Guard from Lieutenant The Honourable Archibald Hamilton (Coldstream Guards. Subsequently, I spent almost 15 years with him on the Conservative benches of the House of Commons. He is now The Lord Hamilton. He was so tall that I felt certain that I spied snow a-top his bearskin cap!). The covering of about six inches of snow had been removed from the lawn to allow the traditional parade to take place for public viewing.

It was an uneventful day, although I did receive a kind invitation from the Commandant, to attend a large dinner to be given that night by the Royal Fusiliers. (If memory serves, I think, at the time, they boasted more officers of General rank than any regiment in the British Army). I attended the dinner, which was a very grand affair. I believe we ate off the service that the Duke of Wellington had presented to the Regiment. I made friends with three young Territorial Fusilier officers sitting near me. As ten o'clock drew near, I took my leave of the Colonel of the Fusiliers and prepared myself for the Ceremony of the Keys.

The Keys Ceremony went well, but the Colonel of the Royal Fusiliers had inadvertently left his hat behind. To acknowledge my salutes he nodded his head—to all eight of my sword movements, which caused some laughter among the onlookers. We then retired to the Officers' mess. I got on so well with three particular Territorial officers that I invited them up to my apartment for more drinks after the main party had broken up. We talked into the night.

At about 12.30 am, one of them, a Judge, rose from his chair saying, "I must be on my way. I have to hear a case in Bristol at ten o'clock this very morning." I escorted them all to the main gate.

Normally, the Yeomen Warders allowed special guests to leave by way of a small wicket gate. On this occasion however, a recently recruited Warden was on duty. Sadly, he did not know the 'form' and was blowed if he was going to accept any unauthorized instructions from the young Officer of the Guard. It was all most embarrassing as the Judge and his companions, who were bankers, pleaded with him and remonstrated to me. Clothed only in their scarlet mess kits, they were getting very cold. I suggested we retire to my rooms.

Once back in my flat, we reviewed the situation. It was bleak. I suggested that they call their wives to explain their predicament. One conversation gave rise to considerable mirth. It ran something like this, "Hello, Darling. I know you may not believe this, but I'm locked in the Tower of London."
He told us afterwards that she had said, 'Don't be

ridiculous! I know you're in the Bag of Nails. Come home immediately!'

"No! No, my dear, I am *not* in the Bag of Nails! Truly, I'm not, Darling. I know it is unbelievable, but I am actually locked in the Tower of London. It's absolutely true. I am here with two other officers, one of whom is a Judge no less, and we are *all* locked in the Tower of London."

'I know you've been drinking. Stop being so stupid and come home at once!' she is alleged to have replied.

"Look, I'll let you speak to the officer of the guard himself." With that, I tried to calm the distraught woman. To help me, I even resorted to putting the Judge on the telephone. Eventually, she was placated, or sort of. Her shrill voice became more of a whimper. But, it has to be said, it was still a whimper of disbelief.

By far the worst situation was that of the Judge. The more he explained his predicament, the more I realized that something had to be done and soon. He just *had* to be in Court in Bristol later that morning. But, what could we do? As I explained to my 'guests', even in those days, the Tower of London was a very secure location housing, as it did, the priceless Crown Jewels. I decided to go on a reconnaissance patrol to test the security. As I did not want to 'spook' the sentries and the fact that I was the only one with a great coat on a very cold night, I decided to go alone.

As I descended the steps of the Officers' mess my eyes fell on the Chapel Royal, to my front. I immediately thought of the bell rope and how useful it would be for scaling walls, but which walls and where? I found a relatively easy route out of the inner battlements, via what is now the 'Queen Elizabeth' arch. All it required was to avoid being seen by one sentry at the extreme end of his beat. Once in the Casemates, I found a stone stairway between the front door of a small house and the Well tower. It led to the roof of some Yeoman Warders' houses that abutted the outer battlements. The stairway was barred by a large iron gate of vertical bars. It would have been very difficult to scale. The lock was caked with black paint, but I tried it. Fortunately, with a little force, it opened and I climbed the stone staircase slowly and very quietly. Once on the flat roof, I noticed a chimney stack that rose close to the outer battlement. It would make a good anchor-base to loop the rope around. The top of the outer battlements was some eight to ten feet above the roof. It also had an inwards facing overhang, or cover, which would make it extremely difficult to scale. However, I also noticed that the stair well wall offered a useful potential launch pad that could be used, in a team effort, to climb onto the top of the outer battlement. So after all, it did look just possible for my 'guests' to get into the grass moat, some thirty or forty feet below. From there they would have to find their own way out to the City, probably along the line of the river Thames. After all, I thought to myself, 'they were active Territorial officers in a fine regiment. They will be relatively easy for me to organise into a team and they would surely have a considerable store of initiative, as a group, when left alone in the moat. Yes, this is possible, provided we are very careful and quiet, when the snow will help us.' My guests were clearly not very fit and their physical strength to weight ratio did give me cause for some concern, but at least they would be going *down* the rope and not up! They would also be highly motivated.

I returned to find a way into the Chapel. On my way I had to wait, hidden in the shadows, while a sentry completed his beat. In that time I began to have second thoughts as to whether it was decidedly bad form or even blasphemous for me to take the bell rope from a church. Furthermore, the rope might be very old and not up to the weight of a body, especially the bodies of somewhat overweight retired officers. It might also be too short, for the bell tower is not that tall. As I walked through the snow along the side of the main parade ground, past the White Tower, my eyes fell upon the chain that held the public back. I tested it and found that it could be detached from the posts. I detached some of it and measured off what I though was a reasonable amount to allow for both the thirty plus foot height of the battlements and a loop around the chimneystack. I then joined it up, remembering my Boy Scout reef knots, and left it in four piles that I calculated each of us was capable of carrying. Chain is deceptively heavy and I knew that, as my guests had no overcoats or gloves, I had to do the maximum preparatory work myself, leaving as little as possible to them and to chance. Furthermore, I was legitimate, they were not. I therefore had to reduce, as far as possible, the time in which they were exposed, in the floodlights, to chance observation by either staff or sentries — my sentries!

I returned to my rooms to find three very dejected looking officers. I told them of my plan and their faces lit up, partly I thought because they sensed freedom, but partly because they may have fancied some adventure, This last thought worried me a little, for the implications of failure were, for me and my career, very serious indeed.

At first, they thought it was overkill and mildly ridiculous, but I knew that rehearsal was vital, especially for the final vault onto the parapet of the battlements. After some laughs they came round to my view. I explained the career risk I was taking for them. This helped to focus their attention. I took very great pains to draw out my plans on paper. Due to the essential need for stealth, I took the precaution of rehearsing them, particularly in carrying the chain, all joined together (tying knots in sticky, ice-cold chain in the dark was not a task to leave to chance); action on freezing against a wall, to avoid the gaze of the sentry, or anyone else; an alibi (officers' high jinks), if apprehended; the looping of the chain around the chimney stack; the assisted launch of each person onto the parapet overhang; the gentle lowering of the chain over the wall; and, finally, both the order and method of climbing down the chain, with the least fit man last, so that his friends could help him from below, if he slipped. I then gave them advice on how to conduct themselves and drew them a suggested route that they should follow, to best avoid sentries, once they were in the moat. I nominated one of them, the Judge, who appeared to command the most respect, as their commander, so there would be no unnecessary argument, on the ground. They, especially the Judge, were thrilled to find any solution whatsoever. They were therefore increasingly keen to obey. I had no arguments. We did several rehearsals. With each dry run, the laughs decreased and they improved to become a really quite well drilled patrol, even by Grenadier standards! Finally, we warmed our uniforms on the central heating pipes.

We stole out onto the floodlit parade ground. My guests looked apprehensive, but resplendent against the snow in their scarlet mess kits. We lined up and picked up our individual piles of joined chain. I checked to see that each could in fact carry his load satisfactorily. It is amazing how expectations of escape fire the adrenalin. We moved off in single file. I have to say that, despite the severe career strain I was under, I did smile when I saw our floodlit silhouette against various walls. We looked like a severely overloaded chain gang.

We passed the sentry beat without detection and passed the Salt Tower. Once on the roof of the Yeoman Warder's house we had to be very careful not to slip in the snow. The chain was looped around the chimneystack and lowered over the wall, as planned. However, the first climber (I had chosen the most athletic looking one) found it very difficult to get a first handgrip of the chain, which lay tight against the top coping stones. After some hairy moments, he was safely down in the moat but, even from the top, I could see that his white stiff shirt was ruined. The chain was extremely rough to climb, even downwards. The second officer followed without mishap. I felt so sorry for the third and most overweight officer that I gave him my white kid gloves. It was a gift that was to cause me great pain soon afterwards. Despite my gloves he had a difficult descent. As planned, the other two helped him over the last yard or so as he found his feet. Smiling, they waved up the 'all clear'. My relief was short lived, however.

I reached down, with gloveless hands, to pull up the chain. It would not budge. It had taken three of us to lower it with relative ease. I was now on my own and pulling it *up!* As I knelt on the parapet my heart sank. I wondered what to do. I even allowed myself a non golf-like negative thought - the thought that this would be a fine moment for some journalist to be passing in his motor car over Tower Bridge to see the Officer of the Guard apparently lowering a rope over the defences. What a story it would have made in the tabloids! As I came to my senses I stripped off my overcoat and tied the sleeves around part of the chain and pulled. With the increased leverage, I was successful. After a few repetitions I was able to pull the remaining chain up by hand. I then had to lower the chain back onto the roof. The cold was really getting to my hands and I let some chain slip. Sadly it landed where we had been standing on the roof, having trampled down the snow. With no snow cushion, it landed with a dull crash. However it was enough of a noise to cause alarm. Through the skylight I saw an electric light go on. Out came a person (a Yeoman Warder?) carrying a torch. I froze. Despite the electric light he shone his torch around in the landing, but appeared satisfied that nothing was wrong. It was a real scare and made me take far more care in climbing down to the roof. Guards' mental discipline was needed and came to the fore, thank God.

Once through the gate it took me four strenuous trips to get the chain back to the parade ground. Thank God, I was fairly fit in those far off days. I then had to secure it to the posts. I returned to my room to put my hands in warm and then hot water. I lay down exhausted, wondering what next?

My guests may be in trouble, especially if sighted by one of my sentries or the police. I telephoned the Sergeant of the Guard. Much to his surprise I announced that I wished to go on a round of the sentries in fifteen minutes. "Sir," he said in astonishment, "I'll expect you here in fifteen minutes then, Sir." I made hasty efforts to get out some of the chain stains from my great coat and made my way to the guardroom.

At about 3.00 in the morning the sentries were amazed to see me. I asked them all if they had seen anything unusual. To my great relief, all the answers were negative. On my return to the guardroom I worried that an incident could be reported and that my Sergeant might, showing great initiative, raise the alarm before telling me. I decided to tell him what had happened. I invited he up to my flat for a drink. It was now about 3.30 am in the morning, but he accepted. More importantly, like most great Guards Non-Commissioned Officers, he saw the funny side. In fact, as no mishap had occurred, he thought it was a good laugh. (No names, no pack drill.)

Just before I went to bed, I received a telephone call from the Judge to say that they had indeed got out through the docks and that all was well. He was full both of thanks and praise. I was filled with relief.

Although my hands ached, I slept very, very well, until the first 'thank-you' calls arrived later in the morning, from the bankers who said they would dine out on their experience for the rest of their lives.

I was too tired to get dressed and watch the opening of the main gate early that morning. However, I'll bet there were more than a few Yeomen Warders, with Minox cameras hidden under their cloaks, just waiting to see three shame-faced officers come out in their scarlet mess kit, as the early public visitors entered, looking astonished!

A few weeks later, I was on Tower Guard again. One senior looking Yeoman Warder, on duty at the White Tower, could scarce contain himself. He approached me as I mounted the Officers' mess steps.

"Excuse me Sir." He said very charmingly. "Weren't you the young officer who had his guests locked in the other night?"

"I could have been. Why do you ask?"

"Oh Sir, nothing official, you understand."

"Tell me more. It sounds interesting," I said fishing for knowledge as to how much he knew.

"Well Sir, a certain young officer in your regiment had three guests locked in here the other night. But in the morning, they were all gone. The whole place has been abuzz to know how he got them out." Then he added with a quizzical smile, "No names, no pack drill, Sir, but was you the young officer concerned, Sir?"

"How interesting. If something comes to mind, I'll let you know," I said with a smile and a wink.

"Yes, please do that, Sir. I have to say, he did look very like you Sir!" He saluted with a knowing smile and returned to his post.

Several years later, I was invited to a dinner party at Queen House, by Lady Butler, wife of the Lieutenant Governor, Colonel Sir Thomas Butler. I remember it as an eventful dinner for two reasons.

First, there was a *son et lumiere* being carried out on the South bank of the river about the very rooms we were in (now, the young trees have grown too high for such a clear view). Floodlights kept flashing onto the windows and we had to avoid movement in front of the windows, while the lights shone.

Secondly, Lady Butler took all the women out after dinner, leaving the men folk to talk, in the customary English manner. Colonel Tom sat at the head of the table with a good cigar and passed the port. After a few moments, a young Coldstream officer (Captain Sir Brian Bartelott Baronet, if I remember correctly) asked, "Do tell me Sir, how many people have ever escaped from the Tower of London?" Colonel Tom drew himself up and also upon his cigar, in clear preparation for a long discourse. Over time, he described several escapes in graphic detail. (I have long forgotten the precise number of escapes he listed, but let us say for sake of argument that it was 'four'). He then summed up by saying, "Well, I think that brings the total to 'four'." Then, taking the cigar from his lips, he looked knowingly and directly into my eyes, adding, "Detected, that is!"

Footnote:
If any of my three escapees read this story, I would be most grateful if they would be kind enough to contact me via Regimental Headquarters. According to Sir Thomas Butler, they are in distinguished company!

HM Tower of London.

Old Officers Mess
(the home of 'real' ghosts)
now a museum
(with only stories of ghosts)

CASEMATES - HM Tower of London
showing 'escape route', iron gate and steps leading to roofs
of Wardens' houses

Chapter 14

Dirty Gloves

Wellington barracks, 1963

Any person reading the previous few stories could be excused for concluding that, contrary to belief, the Guards lacked discipline in our day. In fact, the discipline was always relatively strict, some would say very strict, as is shown partially by the following story.

In the winter of 1963, Captain John Magnay, our Adjutant, and I had been invited to a wonderful weekend house party by Mrs. Elizabeth Pitman for the Wire Fund dance of the Duke of Beaufort's Hunt, near my home. I was looking forward to it, especially as I thought a lot of her daughter, Lavinia.

During the week preceding the dance, I was the Subaltern of the Buckingham Palace Guard. We changed in the old Officers' mess at Wellington barracks. The officer commanding the Tower of London Guard, the Ensign of the Queen's Guard and I put on our Bearskin caps and white gloves in the entrance hall. I noticed, in passing, that some contract workers were cleaning the brass work of the hall.

We marched out to the parade ground and up to the Adjutant, Captain John Magnay. As we saluted him, he looked askance at my right hand glove and said very gruffly, "Mr. Browne, your glove is dirty. Its not just dirty, it's black! Attend my memoranda the day after you dismount guard."

"Sir," I replied, disheartened. After the Adjutant had finished inspecting us, I began 'marching the ground' with the Tower Guard commander. As I did so, I glanced down at the palm of my right hand glove. To my dismay, I found that John Magnay was absolutely correct. My beautiful white kid glove was indeed black. It was all very embarrassing. As I marched, I wondered just how it could possibly have happened, when my gloves were fresh from the cleaners. Then I fluffed. The contract cleaner must have forgotten to wipe the brass cleaner off the handle I used to open the door. It was unfortunate, very unfortunate.

Two days later, I attended the Adjutant's memorandum, as instructed. John Magnay gave me three days extra Picket Officer, on the grounds that an officer is always responsible for the condition of his kit. I respected John Magnay's argument and his integrity. However, his punishment prevented me from attending the dance with him. Mrs. Pitman was less than amused when I telephoned her to cancel, at some 24 hours notice. She did however remain a good friend, for her late husband and both her sons, Giles and Hugh, had been in the Blues and she knew the form of the sometimes harsh discipline in the Household Brigade. As for dear Lavinia, she married my Sandhurst compatriot, The Lord Fermoy, also in the Blues.

Footnote:
1. William Saunders told me of a similar incident of 'officer discipline' regarding gloves, in the First Battalion at the old Chelsea barracks. On his way to attend a parade, he did up the button of one of his white gloves as he descended the stone steps of the Officers' mess, which abutted onto the parade ground. His action did not escape the eagle eyes of the Adjutant, Captain Bernard Gordon-Lennox. On Adjutant's Memoranda, the next day he received two extra piquet's for being 'improperly dressed for parade!'

2. In later years, I remembered my painful lesson. As Secretary of the Conservative Defense Committee, I was always wary of the new idea of 'contracting out' and the lowering of standards by stealth!

Chapter 15

A Ghost at the Tower of London?

HM Tower of London, 1963.

I had never seen or sensed a ghost. However, I did not totally dismiss the notion of ghosts. I had long been aware of the many ghost stories at the tower of London.

Some months after the 'great escape' of my three guests, the Officers' mess at the Tower of London had been closed and was being gutted in preparation for a major renovation. However, one set of rooms was kept habitable for the Officer of the Guard. I have to admit that, even in the daylight, it was quite spooky. It was a very large, old building. Most of the floors were ripped up, builders' equipment and dust were everywhere and naked light bulbs offered minimum illumination.

Late that night, I had returned from a round of the sentries. I entered the tomb-like Officers' mess. Every step I took seemed to echo round the entire building. I got to my room, brushed my teeth and went to bed.

Having turned the light out, I was half asleep, when I thought I could hear footsteps. I listened very attentively. Yes, I could definitely hear footsteps. My God, I thought, 'This is not a movie. This is the Tower of London and I know I am the only person in the entire building'. But the steps went on. I pinched myself. Still they shuffled slowly on. I sat up and turned on my bedside light. Still they went on, now more clearly on the floor immediately above me.

Feeling decidedly rattled, I put on my dressing gown and house shoes. I grabbed my only weapon, my trusty sword. I then followed the shuffling steps, echoing eerily from the floor above. The echo was unsettling to say the least, especially in the murky half-light. Then they started, very slowly, down the dimly lit staircase. I flattened myself against the wall at right angles to bottom of the staircase. When I judged the steps were almost upon me, I leapt out in the 'on guard' position. I was stunned. There was a man, also in a dressing gown and pajamas. He fell back with a gasp, and an expression of fear and utter shock on his face. He slid gently down the last few stairs to my feet, with my sword pointed at his stomach. We both looked at each other in complete amazement for several seconds. I found that I was shaking. After a moment, I regained my normal voice and asked, " What the hell are you doing here?"

"Well, who… who… who are you?" he replied, stuttering somewhat.

"I'm the Officer of the Guard," I said, petulantly.

"Oh, you're not a Fusilier then?"

"No, I 'm a Grenadier"

"Well, I'm a Fusilier. I've just returned from overseas. I slept though the afternoon and have just woken up. I was just trying to find some brother officers, but all the rooms are empty."

"We need a drink," I replied. Lowering my sword I added, "come to my room" He very willingly agreed. I helped him up and we each gulped down a large whisky. We enjoyed a good laugh as we relived the event.

Chapter 16

"Just a Few Screws Loose, Constable. That's All"

Buckingham Palace, June 1963

When subaltern of the Buckingham Palace Guard, we messed with the Captain and the Ensign at Saint James's Palace. Grenadiers originally wore caps trimmed with fur, ultimately evolving into the bearskin. In hot weather, I used sometimes to take a couple of bottles of beer in my bearskin cap, for the Gold Sergeant and Lance Sergeant in the Buckingham Palace guardroom. Loading up was quite tricky. Like drinking a 'yard of ale' (as we learned to do on our parachute course) the final beer comes in a great rush. It is very easy to 'brain' oneself in putting on a bearskin cap with two full bottles of beer inside it!

n one hot June night, I decided to take some beer back to Buckingham palace, in my bearskin cap, for the two Sergeants.

Everything went well. However, this was a particularly still night, like the calm before a thunderstorm. All was completely still. It was very late and the traffic was almost non-existent. As I marched towards Buckingham Palace I began to realize that I could hear the two bottles clinking together.

As I entered the Gateway, into the forecourt of Buckingham Palace, the duty policeman looked a little taken a back and indeed concerned. He looked at me and said, " Are you alright, Sir?"

"Oh yes, I'm fine thank you, Constable."

"Are you quite sure, Sir?" he pleaded, looking very concerned and up at my bearskin cap.

"Just a few loose screws, Constable, that's all," I replied with a smile and a wink.

"Oh, I see Sir. Very well," he replied smiling.

Officers, 2nd Battalion, Grenadier Guards
Visit of the Colonel, Maj-Gen Sir Allan Adair, Bt
Hubbelrath, Germany, 1961

Part Four

British Guiana, with the Second Battalion

June 1963 to March 1964

British Guiana was remote, so remote that many people had no idea where it was. One had the feeling that this ignorance may have stretched even to the Foreign and Colonial Office, for the colony gave the distinct impression of a certain 'colonial neglect'. Even the maps depicted vast areas of white space with 'unexplored' printed over them. Situated on the Northern coast of South America, just a few degrees off the Equator, it was hot and sticky, with most of its surface covered with tropical jungle. It had a wide alluvial plain in the North, which was where the bulk of the population lived, adjacent to plantations of rice and sugar fields. Sadly, the coastline was covered, not with sand, but with mud, swept down from the river Orinoco, in neighbouring Venezuela. The middle of the country was covered in jungle, but was rich in bauxite, manganese and some diamonds. To the South lay vast prairies, stretching to the Brazilian border and used for cattle ranching.

The original Amerindian settlers had been pushed inland by the early colonialists who planted rice and sugar cane. The plantations initially employed black slaves. Once slavery was abolished they worked the sugar mills exclusively, and hired labourers from India and China replaced them in the fields. The people were basically charming and very easy going. Sadly however, racial competition reared its ugly head between the two largest groups: the Blacks, led by Forbes Burnham, and the Indians, led by Doctor Cheddi Jagan, whose American wife, Janet, was reputed to be a Communist. In the early 1960's racial tensions rose to the point of racially motivated bomb killings and murders. In late 1962, the 1st Battalion, Coldstream Guards were sent out as the resident British battalion, to act in aid of the Civil Power. In early 1963, we, as the 2nd Battalion, Grenadier Guards, were detailed to take over from them in June/July. We were stationed at Caterham, conducting intensive Public Duties, including the provision of two Guards on that year's Queen's Birthday Parade. We were briefed and the Advanced Party, under Major Miles Lambert (formerly Guards Parachute Company) was prepared to leave immediately after the Birthday Parade. In the meantime, the situation in British Guiana worsened and a total, countrywide strike was initiated.

As a battalion of some 700 men we were deployed to keep order in a country of almost the same geographic area as that of Great Britain. Talk about overstretch; it actually offered great opportunity for truly independent command at junior levels and that was great fun.

Our posting to British Guiana, or BG as it was called locally, turned out to be a momentous one. You either loathed it or loved it. As a ten month posting, it was particularly hard on the married men. For some of the unmarried men it was 'El Dorado', for rum was cheap, the evenings sultry and most BG girls were anxious to get out of the country by marring a British soldier. It would be their one-way ticket to heaven, or so they thought! Whatever your state, BG was unique.

BG proved to be such a memorable posting that, on Sunday 22nd June 2003, the 1st Guards Club held a reunion at Lord Rollo's home in Berkshire. There were only two absentees: Charles Acland (in Australia) who donated a dozen bottles of

Dom Perignon, and Desmond Evans (our Paymaster, and ill in Wales) who donated several bottles of Kirsch. The whole event was superbly organized by Philip Wright and David Rollo. Appropriately bathed in sunshine, the party started following Sunday church at 11.00 am. After a superb and ever so slightly alcoholic luncheon, to the accompaniment of 'jump-up' music, the 'Loyal Messages' were read out by our BG Adjutant, John Magnay (formerly Guards Parachute Company). There followed an afternoon of BG films, videos and decidedly youthful merriment. The whole affair finally closed at midnight. Sadly, the Regimental golf tournament was the following day. Our scores reflected a 'reunion party *extraordinaire*'. In my experience it was indeed extraordinary for such an epic reunion party to take place for a peacetime posting. Normally, such reunions are reserved exclusively for the experience of the stunning events and the enhanced comradeship of high intensity war. It is safe to say that BG was truly an epic posting.

As the Signals Officer I was detailed for the Advanced Party. I was also a Subaltern on one of the four Guards that the Grenadiers found, that Summer, on the Queen's Birthday Parade. I had spare time enough only to attend a friend's wedding and carry out my duties as Best Man. In just a day or two after the parade, we were out of our scarlet tunics and into desert coloured khaki drill. We left Heathrow on an Eagle Airways turbo-prop aeroplane, bound for a refueling stop in Bermuda. We were *en route* to British Guiana. In those days, that was fast moving.

The Advanced Party was very ably commanded by Major Miles Lambert, (then commanding the Inkerman Company). The second in command was Captain the Honourable Jeremy Monson. From memory, also included were: the Intelligence Officer, Captain Michael Healing; Captain Martin Lockhart Smith; Assistant Adjutant, Captain Richard Proes; Lieutenant Quartermaster and Transport officer, Fred Clutton MBE, MM; and Quartermaster, Lieutenant Lou Drouet MBE, (Badly shot-up in the Italian campaign, Lou was outstandingly 'good news' and a physically very powerful Grenadier. I last saw him when he was in charge of the Bisley rifle ranges. He ran our Lord v

Commons annual rifle shoot for the magnificent Visianagram trophy. This was, in my day, superbly organized by my friend Michael Colvin MP (Grenadier Guards). It was very good to see former Sergeant Major Lou Drout 'lick' our ragged band of politicians into shape in rapid order and thereby give us all a great deal more fun.

BRITISH GUIANA, 40th Reunion Party
'Diamond' estate table, at Lord Rollo's home.
22nd June 2003

Chapter 17

Bermuda—
A Monson Refuelling Party

Bermuda, 15th June 1963

*I*n the jet age it is sometimes hard to remember the relative discomfort of piston engine, or ever turbo-prop flight. The noise, the vibration and the relatively short range are things of the past. On 15th June 1963 we trundled our way across the Atlantic for what seemed like endless hours in an overcrowded Britannia turbo-prop aeroplane. We looked forward to our refuelling stop in Bermuda; we would have looked forward to it even more if we had any idea of what awaited us. Before we started our descent, Jeremy Monson let it be known his mother, The Dowager Lady Monson, was flying up from her home in Jamaica to give us a cocktail party at Bermuda airport.

Upon landing, we straightened our crumpled khaki drill uniforms and made for the main airport building. Once inside, we found that Lady Monson had taken over the entire airport lounge. (It is exactly the same room today.) Hospitality was on a lavish scale. Lady Monson had set up a massive bar for the men, a bar for the Sergeants' mess and, at the far end, an Officers' bar. For many of us, it was to be our first introduction to rum - West Indian rum. It went down like lemonade and, after our long flight, we were thirsty. After about an hour, it was time to walk back to our aeroplane. But, by this time, the rum was beginning to kick-in, like a mule! We moved back. It would be misleading to say that we marched. Luckily it was dark, for many tottered and some were half carried, but we all made it aboard. The remainder of the flight was near oblivion for most of us. Apparently, we passed through a very violent storm in which the aeroplane was struck, dropping several thousand feet. None of us turned a hair!

Incidentally, Lady Monson is alive and just a few days from her century. I do hope she sees this appreciative account of the epic party she gave for The Regiment.

Soon after daybreak we landed at Atkinson airfield, the BG national airport. After we had taxied, our aircraft was pushed, by hand into its exact unloading position by men of the Coldstream Guards. The total strike was biting! We were greeted by Lieutenant-Colonel Alan Pemberton, Commanding 1st Battalion Coldstream Guards (later, Colonel Alan CVO, MBE). He looked so young and fit. I thought he was their Adjutant. In fact, the Adjutant was Captain John Pilley. It was exhilarating to be met by so many old Coldstream friends from Caterham, Sandhurst and London. In particular, it was good to see close old friends such as Willie Rous (from whom I was taking over as Signals Officer); Julian Pope; Anthony Cordle and Richard Macfarlane. (Later, in 1965, I invited Richard to the Grenadier Waterloo Ball at Windsor, along with Louisa Babington-Smith. It proved to be the most successful and the most wonderful of my match-making efforts. They are still very happily married and still live in my old parliamentary constituency. I trust they voted the 'right' way!). We were given an excellent Coldstream breakfast, presided over by Captain Hugh Middelton (now, The Lord Middelton) sitting at the head of the table, like Long John Silver, with a huge, blue and yellow Macaw on his shoulder. We then drove up to Georgetown for some reconnaissance. We were housed in requisitioned houses in the city.

For the next month we had a wonderful time, under command of the Coldstream and our own Miles Lambert. There were no drills or extra pickets and much interesting information and some dramatic events to assimilate.

One such dramatic event concerned a young Coldstream officer (Second- Lieutenant David Thornewell). He was responsible for the security of the large, isolated town of New Amsterdam, on the far side of a major river. Apparently, one night, a crowd developed outside the main cinema. A large gang, armed with fearsome 'panga' sugar cane cutlasses, tried to attack the cinema crowd. Thornewell deployed his relatively few men, in the dark, to meet the threat. With some of his men he was cornered in a dark alleyway by angry cutlass wielding rioters. Standing in front of his men, he shouted cautionary Warning Orders. They went unheeded. The gang closed in again and he fired one round. This single shot, from our new 7.62 Self Loading Rifle, at point blank range, blew the first man almost apart, a chunk out of the second, went clean through a third and ended in the leg of a fourth. The first two died instantly and the third died later. This news travelled round on the bush telegraph almost faster than on our wireless sets. However, PC officials in London made hitherto unprecedented attempts to Court Martial poor young Thornewell for murder, as a political token. Luckily, The Major General, Sir John Nelson, to his eternal credit (I understand even threatening his resignation), stood firmly and loyally behind the politically scapegoated Coldstream officer and Whitehall beat a 'quiet' retreat. I tremble to think what would happen today.

The event may have been forgotten in Whitehall but it was remembered vividly in BG. Once, one of our ration truck drivers rescued himself and the rations from a civilian, 'stop and steal' ambush on a bridge, using women and children sitting and lying on a bridge, to stop the vehicle. He merely showed that he was armed, cocked his Sterling Sub-Machine gun, allowing a cartridge to fall out, to show that it was loaded, and the would-be looters melted away.

Months later, John Magnay and I, were on a eight-day jungle trek to the Kaieteur Falls and back, with an Amerindian guide. It was quite difficult jungle country. The easiest movement was near or along rivers. However, when we were anywhere near rivers we would run into groups of 'Porknockers' or diamond hunters. They were very rough people and this was remote jungle. Murders would not even be noticed, let alone reported or solved. We were only three in number and very tired. But, we knew we were not dealing with motivated troops, only with lay-about potential robbers and killers. So, in order to discourage 'interference' at night, we would merely toss a piece of wood into the river and fire a few rounds at it. We were never approached, thanks to the reputation of our Coldstream advertised 'vunder' weapon.

Soon, our very happy month with the Coldstream was over and our main body arrived from England.

Individual killings and bomb explosions continued for a while. One new tactical problem was that of Riot Control. We had all been trained to cope with rioters who were on foot, such as in Cyprus. BG presented us with a new type of rioter, on a bicycle! While BG rioters were far less intimidating than the Cypriots, they were far more mobile and used their mobility to good effect. We had to smash their bicycles. At last, we could see a practical, tactical reason behind all that stamping of feet in the Army. Whoever designed the drill was prescient: it was perfect for destroying the spokes of bicycle wheels and so reducing the maddening mobility of our riotous foe!

A few weeks later, we were reinforced by a battalion of the 60th Kings Royal Rifle Corps. (A wonderful regiment, originally founded in America, with some 4,000 men in 4 battalions, before the Revolution in 1755, as the 62nd and then the 60th Royal American Rifles. I believe it is the only British regiment to have contained the word 'American' in its official title). It was good to see them and to meet a number of Green Jacket friends, including my former study companion from Malvern, a very fine young officer, Lieutenant Christopher Bullock (now, Brigadier Christopher, OBE, MC).

When in BG we had visits from our London District Commander, Major General Sir John Nelson and from our Regimental Lieutenant-Colonel, Colonel Anthony Way, MC.

Chapter 18

The 'Star' Signal Patoon

British Guiana, July 1963

It is said that the three great army commands are a Platoon, a Regiment and a Division. The signal platoon is a wonderful command in any regiment. I was extremely lucky in that my Commanding Officer, Colonel 'Fanny' Jefferson and my Adjutant, Captain John Magnay, were both former Signals Officers. They both knew how vital communications were to command and control; how difficult they could be in certain types of terrain and that success depended critically upon both the quality and practice of all operators. In short, I had that essential support from the top. This translated into three crucially beneficial decisions.

First and foremost, it was decided that I should have a full strength platoon of some 50 all ranks (2 officers, 15 Non Commissioned Officers and some 33 Guardsmen), including an Assistant Signals Officer and a Gold Sergeant, in addition to the customary peacetime establishment of a Colour Sergeant. That, in itself, was a great privilege in an all-regular, peacetime army.

Secondly, it was decided to go for quality. I was to be given the pick of three intakes of keen young Guardsmen straight from the Guards depot.

Thirdly, despite our being on Public Duties, I was to be given a block period, of some 6 weeks, away from the battalion in which to get my new platoon together and trained. This again was a very great privilege in a London District battalion, overstretched on Public Duties. I was thrilled to bits at my good fortune when a fourth major positive loomed into view. We were to go to British Guiana, where communications were both very difficult and vital. Indeed, at the height of the General Strike, the battalion communications were almost the only effective communications in the entire country. Furthermore, I would be taking over from my great friend Lieutenant Willie Rous (Coldstream Guards). We were at Sandhurst together and on the same Small Arms and later the same Signals Officers' courses at the School of Infantry, Hythe). I knew he would brief me very well as to what was needed. All in all, I was a very happy trooper.

From memory, my new signal platoon included the following 47 members (I apologise, most sincerely, to any stars whose names or roles I have disgracefully allowed to slip my memory, or whose names or roles I have remembered incorrectly):

2nd Lieutenant	Michael Westmacot Assistant Signals Officer
Colour Sergeant:	(Ernie) Mitchell (later, CSM, Sp Coy)
Gold Sergeant:	(Pete) Hazel (later CSM, Sp Coy)
Lance Sergeants:	'Gus' Creamer (Pln 'Father', i/c stores, later, C/Sgt) Nicholas 'Red' Skelton (Dispatch Rider (DR) / i/c No 1 Coy Sigs -now in Devon) Maurice 'Mo' Joyce (later CQMS SigsWg S of Inf and then, as Lieutenant Colonel, QM at RMAS) Harry Grime (i/ c No 1 coy Sigs) Roy Hobbs (later, GSgt, Squad Instr at Gds Depot) Gerry Chamberlain (Sigs center, i/c No 2 coy Sigs then, Comd Offr's op. Later CQMS Tac HQ Belfast and a Platoon

Commander in No 1 Coy.
His maternal Grandfather fought as a
Grenadier on the Somme (2nd Bn). His
Paternal Grandfather, in the Royal
Artillery, was in direct support of those
Grenadiers.
Mick Harrison (Superb D R. Died tragically
in BG)
Colin Bishop.

Corporals:	Paddy Hanna (i/c batteries vital role with 24/7 ops.)
	David Marshall (later CSM, Army School, Arborfield)
	Bradley Atkinson (later, C/Sgt Rations. Sadly died)
	Franck Hinton (Wife later worked on staff at Buckingham Palace).
	'Ginger' O'Sullivan
Guardsmen:	Jeff Turland (Battalion rugby team-later policeman)
	Trevor 'Trev' Pittam (radio op. Lives in S. Croydon)
	Corbett (Radio op)
	Allan Bossom (crack TG, Morse code operator)
	Allan Edmunds (later, WO Sigs, S of Inf. Warminster)
	Russon (Excellent Bn Boxer-Light Welter weight)
	Greg Wright (crack TG operator. Later C/Sgt)
	Nick Wright BEM (Coffin Bearer -Sir WS Churchill-Later, Gold Sergeant).
	Mal Surman BEM (Coffin Bearer-Sir WS Churchill. Later, City Police. Died)
	Harry Fowler (later Surry Police)

Tiny Seaton
Mick Bennett (Batteries-Vital role in BG
    with Bn net operating for 24 hrs/ 7days
    a week for 10 months. Later, Gold Sgt)
Joe Beaston
Andy Brookes
Ken Poxon
Jeff Brockelhurst
'Trog' Truffet
Jeff Hewson
Steve Collins
'Scottie' Scott
Gough
Titley
Mick Battle (now living in Eastborne)
Bentley
Edwards
King (lineman)
'Doc' Booth (stores)

As a result of the total strike, the signal platoon provided a full range of key communications, including wireless, telephone, dispatch riders and morale sustaining movies, sometimes even for key civilian stations. The flat nature of the land and the jungle cover led to severe 'attenuation' or weakening of wireless signals. There was no high ground suitable for the establishment of a WHF automatic 'rebroadcast station', such as Mount Olympus provided us, in the 1st Battalion, in Cyprus. Added to this, we had regular interference from weather, such as severe tropical thunderstorms. We had, therefore, to depend largely on 'old fashioned' High Frequency radios, like the 62 set and the use of 'sky-wave' antennae. We also had to rely upon Morse code, especially at night. All in all, it was a very full and severe test for a regimental signal platoon. The decision by Colonel 'Fanny' Jefferson and Captain John Magnay to boost the signal platoon saved the day. The signal platoon was outstanding and composed of stars. A definitive mark of the truth of this bold claim is that the battalion wireless net operated, in Morse code, at 16 words a minute (over one character per second and equal to the passing out level for

Signal Officers at the School of Infantry at Hythe). With crack operators such as Lance Sergeants 'Mo' Joyce (now a Lieutenant-Colonel), Gerry Chamberlain, Harry Grime, Roy Hobbs and Nick Skelton; and with Guardsmen Greg Wright and Allan Bossom, the speeds reached an amazing 26 words per minute. With a 'vertical', as opposed to a 'side swiper' (semi-automatic) tapping key, these speeds were exemplary. Indeed, I doubt if these speeds have ever been achieved by any NATO regimental signal platoon since 1945, maybe never. It truly was a star platoon, even by Grenadier standards.

The main Signal Centre was based at Camp House in Georgetown. We had a relay station, with a special high radio mast, at Atkinson Field, and signallers with all Company headquarters (at sugar estates such as: Buxton, Diamond, LBI, Lussignan and Ogle), and even at some outlying Platoon areas such as Rose Hall and New Amsterdam. In addition, I posted signallers with the Royal Naval 'guard ship' and with some of the civilian mining outposts (Alcan and Reynolds Metals) such as Mackenzie, and Kwakwane. The Guardsmen were more than popular in the civilian Out Stations. They represented armed protection against local insurrection at the mines and contact with the outside world. The signallers were spoiled rotten by the local mining people and their families, being given such luxuries as housing, refrigerators and even motor cars. They were also much admired as fit young men. I had to rotate them regularly, not for their morale, but for their health!

I remember being at my desk in the Signals Centre when a major world event occurred. The news came through that President John F. Kennedy had been shot a few minutes earlier, in Dallas, Texas. I immediately had the news sent to Colonel 'Fanny', battalion headquarters and to all the company and outlying platoon locations as well as the civilian substations, on our net. The next day we received instructions from Regimental Headquarters that the Royal Court was to go into 14 days of Official Mourning. As members of the greater Royal Court we, as Household officers, had to wear black armbands and to cancel all celebratory events. The only event to survive was the Military Tattoo that we were in charge of and was for local civilian consumption. Interestingly, the American Air Force officers, based at Atkinson Field, had no such restrictions. (Another most important item that I remember we relayed to the outback was that Captain Martin Lochhart Smith's wife, Margaret, had just given birth to a son and heir).

Chapter 19

Team Spirit

Mackenzie Field, Winter 1963

In a London District battalion it is usually very difficult to get all the members of any team together for competition matches. When overseas this sometimes changed. However, in BG, our battalion was spread out over a very wide area, covering several thousand square miles. On the other hand, our Commanding Officer, Lieutenant-Colonel Francis 'Fanny' Jefferson, was keen on sport, particularly rugby. Added to this, one of the most motivational and charming of Grenadiers and an experienced Army rugby player, Drill Sergeant Ray Huggins, was on hand. Furthermore, as a very fit, but positively ancient 35 years old, he was deemed young enough to play, although Colonel 'Fanny' only very grudgingly agreed on that point!

nce the general strike was over in BG and our re-enforcements (60th Rifles) had arrived, we started to have some spare time and certain minds turned towards rugby football.

Ray Huggins not only knew the game well, but also knew exactly who in our battalion was any good. He even persuaded Lance Sergeant Alan Hughes (an Army hammer thrower) to leave the battalion soccer team for our rugby team! In fairly rapid order we assembled a group to play and selected a team, which we trained very hard. Once we started winning, we trained harder still. I was lucky enough to be the battalion pilot and to have earned the gratitude of a few of the local civilian corporate pilots. This allowed us to bring our team together quickly, from all over the country. We used a superb rugby ground at the Sandbach Parker, Diamond, sugar estate, half way between Georgetown and the airport at Atkinson Field.

The 60th had a very fine team, with Major Peter Welch (if memory serves), a most accomplished officer and former England rugby player as their coach. They had done very well in the Army Cup, before they left for BG as our re-enforcements. In two fierce battles we beat them. We then took on the County level BG team and, in an epic match, beat them also. They were so impressed that they selected five of our team to play for BG against the Trinidad and tobago touring team. In the event, the Grenadiers were the only team to beat the Trinidad and Tobago side. Even Ray Huggins felt that our team was one of the best he had ever played in and certainly the most fun. That was a great compliment because fun is, after all, what all sport should be about. I now list some of the names of this triumphant rugby side. However, I have to admit that, with the passage of almost half a century, I have again disgracefully forgotten some of the very high-grade players we were lucky enough to recruit from our attached staff. I have however, included the names of their Corps. I apologise to them most sincerely. You know, 'growing old is not for the faint hearted'!

Left prop	Drill Sergeant Ray Huggins-Scrum Ldr.
HookerCraftsman	John Woods -REME
Right prop	Guardsman Jeff Turland
Second row-left	Lance-Sergeant Jack Warner
Second row-right	Lance-Sergeant John Campbell
Wing forward-blind	Lance Sergeant Tony Walmesley
Lock	Lance-Sergeant Alan Hughes
Wing forward-open	Captain John Browne- Team Captain
Scrum half	2[nd]Lieutenant Anthony Dennison-Smith
Fly half	Corporal **** ***** RAMC

Wing three Q-Left.	2ndLieutenant Peter Bywater
Center three Q	Lance Corporal **** ****** REME
Center three Q	Lance Corporal **** ****** RAMC
Wing three Q-Right.	Craftsman **** ****** REME
Full back	Lieutenant Philip Wright

2nd Battalion, unbeaten rugby team, BG 1963
Back row (fowards): Woods, Campbell, Warner, Huggins,
Walmesley, Hughes, JB. (Turland, missing)
Front row (backs): *- --, Bywater, Wright,
Dennison-Smith, *- --, *- --, *- --.
(* I apologise sincerely for forgetting the names of these wonderful players)

MALVERN-'Up-Coll' building

Soldering with the US Army, Germany 1961

Entering 'Shooting' phase, Army
Patrol Race, 1961 (Ch 7)

Officers, 2nd Bn Grenadier Guards, training in Yorkshire, 1962.
(Note: Original (Korean style) plain green Combat Kit) (Ch 21)

Bulk of the 'Star' Signal platoon, Caterham, 1963. (Ch 18)

Old Brigade Squad hut, Caterham, 1963. Horse paddock fence line 'used' to lie to left of path. (Ch3)

Sergeant Major Extradinaire: John Lord at Sandhurst in 1963. (Pt 2 & Ch 4)

The unbeaten 2nd Bn Rugby Team, BG 1963.
(Names included in b&w duplicate in text - Ch 19)

2nd Bn Grenadier Guards, Georgetown, BG, November 1963. Signal Platoon of the
Signal Centre and Batallion Headquarters, at Camp house. (Note: Black armband,
reflecting Court Mourning for death of US President J. F. Kennedy) (Ch18)

101

Russian merchant ship; stopped and searched. BG 1964. (Ch 21)

Kaiteur Falls, with our faithful
Amerindian guide. BG 1964. (Ch 17)

State Funeral of Sir W. S. C., 1965. Pall Bearers
await arrival of The Coffin, In foreground, F.M.
Lord Alexander and Lord Atlee. (Ch 23)

Guardsman Sean Povey, on artifical legs, joins JB to inspect Hampshire British Legion Colours Parade, 1990 (Ch 38)

Frederic Winthrop shows memorabilia of his kinsman (in portrait above) to Grenadier Battlefield Tour, 2001 (Ch 41)

'Scoff up', UN armoured car patrol, Cyprus 1965 (Pt 5)

"WHAT THE HELL ARE YOU DOING HERE?"

"ARE YOU A FUSILIER?"

"NO, I'M A GRENADIER"

(Ch 15)

Operation, 'TOP HAT' (Ch 38)

HM Tower of London, Showing outer battlement with 12 ft 'overhang'; chimney stack, around which chain was looped; and skylight in Warden's roof (Ch 13)

That Top Hat again! On 'Monty' with the 'Blue and Buff', Badminton House meet (Ch 38)

(Note: the old American Flag, with very few stars upon it)

GRENADIER GUARDS ASSOCIATION BATTLEFIELD TOUR AND VISIT
TO THE UNITED STATES OF AMERICA 28 SEPTEMBER - 14 OCTOBER 2001

1. Major Michael Giles; 2. Winston Stone; 3. Bernard Robertson; 4. Mary Stone; 5. Ana Robertson; 6. Helen Dummer; 7. Pam Jones; 8. Fred Jones; 9. Maureen Knight; 10. John Crosbie; 11. Shirley Crosbie; 12. John Knight; 13. Unknown; 14. Diana Dawe; 15. Frederick Dawe; 16. John Knott; 17. Mrs Angela Winthrop (host); 18. Frank Browning; 19. Olive Chandler; 20. Joan Woodfield; 21. Brian Scott; 22. Roy Dummer; 23. Mrs Joy Cagiati; 24. Peter Preston; 25. Margaret Preston; 26. Eileen Scott; 27. Isabella Mann; 28. Unknown; 29. Angus Macinnes; 30. Nina Knott; 31. Ruth Wemyss; 32. George Turton; 33. Dixon Wemyss; 34. Major Bob Woodfield, MBE; 35. Graeme Marsden; 36. Mr Frederick Winthrop; 37. Major John Browne; 38. Mrs Suzie Winthrop; 39. Captain Barry Double; 40. Master Thomas Stone.

"DASHED GOOD OF THESE GRENADIER WIVES TO PUT ON SUCH A SUPERB SHOW!"

(Ch 9)

"WHAT THE BLOODY HELL DO YOU THINK YOU'RE DOING IN MY BATTALION AREA?"

(Ch 10)

Chapter 20

"Fire, Fire!"... "Fire, Where, Sir?"

Flying between Georgetown and Rosehall Estate, Winter 1963

When at school at Malvern we had all to join the army section of the Combined Cadet Force, or CCF. However, I was fascinated by the thought of flying. Therefore, once I had completed my basic army training, I transferred to the Royal Air Force section and was lucky enough to become the cadet commander. It was great fun with night flying in two-seater jet fighters, like the NF 14, and even a bomb aimers' course. This section was under the overall command of a wonderful master, George Chesterton, a former wartime Royal Air Force pilot and amateur Worcestershire county cricketer. He was tolerant, charming and inspiring. Under his magic touch my friend and 100 X classmate, Ian MacLaurin (now The Lord MacLaurin, Chairman of Vodaphone, and former Chairman of the England Cricket Board) set what I believe is a record. He played for our school cricket X1 for all of his five years. Ian was in the fine tradition of Malvern batsmen founded by the Fosters and the Days, and perpetuated by such men as Knight, Holme and Legge. Apparently Ian's achievement was unique for the 20th Century - for a 13-year old to face the fast bowling of 18-year olds was indeed formidable. I understand, however, that there is now a boy at Harrow, Sam Northeast, who may well equal this record in the 21st Century.

There were several other wonderful masters at Malvern who undertook the daunting challenge of imparting some education to me. They included Donald Lindsay (an innovative headmaster who 'rifted' Malvern into the 20th century, particularly by giving *academics precedence over sport!); C. Fiddian-Green (Scots Guards); Louis Dodd (Irish Guards); A.Chadder; John 'Tubby' Salter; E. Kennedy (author of the well-known Latin primer); R. Bolam (I fagged for his nephew David who, with a scholarship to Oxford, was killed whilst on National Service with the Royal Hampshire Regiment when leading a patrol in Malaya); H.Wilson (who ran our superb Medical V1th Form); Malcom Staniforth; Cyril Lace; L. Blake (later, Sir Leonard, Baronet); J. 'Twip' Collinson; H.'Jack' Farebrother (my house-master); John Lewis, CBE; Reginald 'Reg' Farrar; R.Stobbs; Norman Rosser; Geoffrey Shaw; Andrew McNair; R. 'Pat' Hooley (who started polo at Malvern); Dennis Saunders (former captain of amateur cup winners 'Pegasus' and a brilliant soccer coach who taught us the new 'possession' style of soccer - introduced to England by the Hungarians in 1953. This took Malvern to the height of schoolboy soccer in our era); and Anthony Leng, DSC, who struggled valiantly to teach me some French.*

Under George Chesterton's guidance I managed to get what was called a 'Flying Scholarship', under which I was trained to fly. I was taught on a Tiger Moth aircraft, at Thruxton, on the edge of my future Parliamentary Constituency of Winchester. As a fully aerobatic biplane, the Tiger Moth was the perfect teaching machine. As 17-year old student pilots, in open cockpits and dressed in leather flying helmets, goggles and flowing scarves, we felt that all that divided us from our hero pilots of the Great War was a brace of machine guns over the aircraft nose! It was the very greatest of fun and we were keen. On our cross-country flights we flew over many military road-convoys and sometimes buzzed them, pretending to shoot them up. They were in desert-sand coloured paint and were en route to the fateful Suez Invasion, in which Grenadier battalions, swelled with reservists, took part.

On arrival in British Guiana in June 1963, my old friend Lieutenant Richard Macfarlane (Coldstream Guards) took me flying in a Piper Cub that he used from Atkinson airfield. On these flights he taught me much about local flying conditions, and how to handle the complete lack of any 'ground control', as the total strike continued.

Once the take-over from The Coldstream Guards was completed, Our Commanding Officer, Lieutenant-Colonel 'Fanny' Jefferson, called an 'Orders Group' which, as his Signals officer, I attended. The subject of transport was raised. Our battalion was deployed over the more populated areas of a jungle country with a geographic size roughly equal to that of Great Britain. The rise of aviation had resulted in the decay of most of the few communication roads that once existed. Wooden bridges, in particular, had collapsed and were left unrepaired. However, the total strike stifled fuel supplies to these civilian aircraft and they ceased to fly. The physical communications, so essential to a Commander, were difficult in the extreme. We had no army aircraft. If my memory serves, the Army Air Corps was then only fledgling. Somewhat in desperation, Colonel 'Fanny' inquired, "Can anybody fly?"

"Sir!" I replied enthusiastically, "I have a Private Pilot's license."

"Can you still fly?"

"Sir, my flying license is current. Provided I am checked out on a particular aircraft within my license limitations, I can fly."

"See me after this meeting and let me hear more."

After the Orders Group had ended, I approached Colonel 'Fanny'.

"Oh Yes, John, so you think you can fly, legally?"

"Sir; I know I can."

"But, even if you can, you're my 'Pronto' (Signals Officer). How can you fit in time to fly?"

"It would fit perfectly, Sir, I have my signallers all over the country and need to visit their signals stations. Richard Macfarlane has already familiarized me with some of the peculiarities of local flying conditions and was kind enough to leave me some scarce fuel. I am also based at battalion headquarters and so largely available to fly for you, Sir."

Colonel 'Fanny' thought for a moment, looked towards his Adjutant, Captain John Magnay, who nodded, and said, "Very well, John, you are now the battalion pilot. Go and find an aeroplane, get checked out and report to me when you're ready."

"Sir!" I said with unbridled enthusiasm.

I drove immediately the 20-odd miles to the private aircraft hanger at Atkinson airfield, where I selected an American twin seated Cessna light aircraft, within my license weight specifications. I wrote out a letter of requisition, on behalf of Her Britannic Majesty (great to be a soldier whilst Marshal Law exists!). I then contacted a flying instructor/pilot, Pat Murphy, who had a particularly attractive daughter whom I knew, at the Bookers Company sugar plantation at Ogle. He agreed to give me some transition training; on aircraft, of course! Within a few days, I arranged for the unemployed Minister of Aviation to 'check me out' in person. (He was grateful to have some flying to do). In the meantime, Captain Fred Clutton, our Quartermaster-Transport Officer, had managed to arrange for some aviation fuel to be shipped in from Trinidad by the Royal Navy. (I subsequently flew to Trinidad to get more signal stores. We flew in an RAF cargo aircraft. There were only two other passengers. On of them was The Right Honourable Duncan Sandys (later, The Lord Sandys), the former Conservative minister and son-in-law of Winston Churchill). Fred Clutton also kindly agreed to have my aeroplane serviced by his Motor Transport platoon (talk about Grenadier flexibility!). Finally, I had some oil drums put out as markers on one of the unused runways at Atkinson. (This provided a period of 'light duties' for those in the detention cells.) I then began to practice my short take-off and landing skills, in preparation for the somewhat short and tight airstrips at most of the sugar estates and jungle camps that I would have to visit. Within a few days I was in business and duly reported back to Colonel 'Fanny'.

He must have been a brave man to entrust his life to a pilot like me. Flying over impenetrable jungle in sometimes threatening weather conditions was not always smooth sailing. I must admit, he did sweat; but I was never quite sure whether this condition was due primarily to the heat or to his concern as to my lack of flying skill! I always hoped it was the former. Anyway, I took him on numerous liaison and reconnaissance fights without mishap. One measure of his courage was that he relaxed himself enough to take numerous photographs!

Like some other young men of those days, I must have become a little cocky over my flying, for I had the temerity to apply to the War Office (now Ministry of Defence) for Flying Pay. It amounted to some seventeen shillings and six pence a day. However, as they say, 'every little counts', especially to an unmarried Captain! My application was greeted with typical Whitehall disdain. I was told that, as I was not an 'officially' qualified army pilot, I was not entitled to flying pay, under any circumstances. When I told Colonel 'Fanny' he was angry. He felt, as I was flying under difficult, even perilous conditions, without any proper back-up or mechanical maintenance, that I not only deserved it, but richly so. He took up my case, with gusto. A few weeks later, a typically mean Whitehall compromise was reached; I was to be granted flying pay, but only on the days upon which I actually flew! It was great to serve under commanders like Colonel 'Fanny'. I was not alone in this feeling, for the morale in the 2nd Battalion at that time was extremely high.

Flying in BG and with Colonel 'Fanny' was not only most interesting, but also the greatest of fun. We did however, have our scary moments. One sunny morning we took off from Atkinson Field bound for the Rosehall estate in the far East of the country. We flew over the vast sugar cane fields of Estates such as Buxton. Diamond, LBI, Lussignan, Ogle and Rosignol, just inland from the coastline. Suddenly, Colonel 'Fanny' called out, "Fire, Fire!"

"Fire? Where, Sir, Where?" I replied in a shrill voice. It was a nasty, almost fatal, situation to be caught on fire in mid-air in a small aircraft. We had no parachutes and the fire-fighting equipment was rudimentary, to say the least. It consisted of one small fire canister under the passenger seat. It was pre-attached to a small pipe that guided the contents directly onto the fuel carburretor. I looked again at my instruments, particularly the oil and temperature gauges. They were fine, but with unskilled maintenance, could not wholly be relied upon.

"I don't know, but I smell fire. It must be here somewhere.

Where's the fire extinguisher!"

"One moment, Sir. We first have to see where it is coming from." I did not say that it was under his seat. "If we detach the fire extinguisher and then find it is in the engine, after all, we'll be in even worse trouble, Sir."

"The smell's getting stronger, now."

"I can't see anything in the cockpit. Can you see any flame coming from the engine on your side, Sir?" I checked my instruments again, looked around the cockpit and then out of the window. There, below me, was a trail of smoke. Luckily however, it was coming, not from our aeroplane, but from the ground. They were burning the sugar cane in one of the fields below, before cutting it. That was the cause of the smell. "We're alright, Sir. There's our fire," I said, pointing and explaining briefly as I did so. We were both greatly relieved. The greatest compliment followed. It was that, our brave Colonel 'Fanny' kept 'a flyin', with me. I said he was brave!

When I returned my aeroplane to its hangar I always left it full of petrol, in readiness for an emergency medical flight. However, on getting the aeroplane out, I naturally, always re-checked the fuel level. Almost invariably it was near empty. Clearly, the petrol was being stolen by other pilots. However, I said nothing. I knew that the civilian companies had urgent and sometimes emergency needs for their flights. This largesse was repaid in spades. Once the general strike was settled, these civilian pilots flew any sortie that I asked for, including the flying of our medical missions, mail, signal spare parts, signallers and even my rugby players, saving me much valuable time and the army much fuel.

Chapter 21

'Stop and Search that Russian Ship'

Demerara River, Georgetown, 1964

Today, it is sometimes hard to remember quite how close to strategic war and annihilation we all actually were in the 40 years following the Second World War. The Cold War was sometimes very cold indeed. Even in December 1985, when I was appointed Parliamentary 'escort' to Mr. Gorbachev on his first visit to the West, I remember being asked for my opinion on Gorbachev by The Right Honourable Sir Geoffrey Howe QC, MP (Foreign Secretary). On the first night of the visit, he came to sit by me, during the 10.00 o'clock Division, in the 'Aye' lobby of the House of Commons and asked, "Well John, how did it go? What do you think of our friend Gorbachev?"

"I think he has the charisma to be the next Soviet Leader. Indeed, he is so self confident that I have the distinct feeling he has secretly been all but approved."

"Really, and what do you think that will mean?"

"I think he will bring about great change."

"John, whatever he is like, we still have to deal with the Nomenklatura (party elite) and they will never allow a major change to take place." The conversation was then interrupted by the Whips' (traditional hunting) cry of "Hounds gentlemen, please" to hurry Members along and to clear the division lobby. Such, with the crucial exception of Margaret Thatcher, whom I briefed subsequently that night, was the mindset of our elite. The World was set fast in the 'ice' of the Cold War'. I was ridiculed in both the British and American media until, on the third day, Margaret Thatcher said, "I think I can do business with this

man." This pivotal strategic statement heralded that the way was then open for Gorbachev to meet President Reagan and to bring an end to the Cold War, which had gripped our entire world for the past four decades.

Back in October 1962, we were on a battalion exercise on the Yorkshire moors (Benman camp, I think). I was in the battalion headquarters' vehicle-tent when dramatic news came through about President Kennedy and the Cuban Missile Crisis. Our Commanding Officer, Colonel 'Fanny' Jefferson, who was not given to overstatement, commented thoughtfully, "I think we are now nearer to world war than at any time since 1945." It was deeply sobering to us all.

*I*n British Guiana (BG), in early 1964, my close friend Captain Michael Healing (Intelligence Officer) came down to my office in camp House. "Close the door," he said. "I have been given a most interesting assignment."

"Like what?"

"Down boy, down boy!"

"Come on Michael, like what?"

"Like the American intelligence services believe that a Russian freighter is approaching Georgetown harbour..."

"A Russian ship?"

"Yes, a Rusky. Supposedly it is carrying arms and ammunition for the training of Cuban terrorists in the North Western jungles of BG. Apparently, the cache is concealed in tomato ketchup boxes."

"Wow!"

"I have been assigned to accompany the Chief of Police with a BG police search Party to stop the ship, to board it and to search it."

"My God, and what if it doesn't stop?"

"We thought of that. We will have four anti-tank guns mounted on the sea wall."

"What Hornblower! To sink a Russian ship?"

" H.E. (our superb Governor, Sir Ralph Gray - subsequently as Lord Gray, my Lord Prior when I was on Chapter General of the Order of Saint John) does not think it'll come to that. But we will need reliable communications, on a special frequency between me, the Governor, the Commanding Officer and the anti-tank guns."

"Ok, I'll set that up myself. Can I come with you?"
"You can come in the police patrol boat, but you can't go aboard the Russian ship. We want a police, not a military profile. I am to be the only soldier to actually board the ship."

"My God, this is big stuff."
"Yes, it certainly is interesting, that's true."

It was quite amazing to me to see how a major incident could arise seemingly out of nowhere. Given the climate of the time, an incident like this could have exploded out of control, in short order. However, I doubted that our Governor would have requested and authorized such action without liaising very closely with the Foreign Office and, through them, with the Americans. Nevertheless, it was somewhat worrying to see just how low were some of the potential melting points of the Cold War.

In the event, the Russian freighter did obey the order to 'Have-too' and to allow our boarding party aboard. Apparently the ship's captain was very surprised, but cooperative. Thankfully, nothing was found and the ship was allowed to proceed to into port.

Footnote:
Michael Healing and I subsequently spent an unforgettable two weeks annual leave in Manaus, on the Amazon and on the Copacabana in Rio de Janeiro. Sadly, he died while I was working on Wall Street in the late 1960s. His dear wife Mandy, was a very great support and comfort to him during his suffering.

2 Company, 2nd Battalion Grenadier Guards
on helicopter exercises with the American Army
Germany, Summer 1961
(Note: new web equipment and SL rifle but still old fashioned
battle dress and gaiters)

Photo by Ronald J. Rayniak

Part Five

CYPRUS, WITH THE FIRST BATTALION

After a short spell at the Guards Depot Pirbright I was posted, in the spring of 1965, to the 1st Battalion in Germany, which were filling a United Nations 'Peacekeeping' role in Cyprus. The Commanding Officer was Lieutenant Colonel Michael Bayley, (later Brigadier Michael, MBE), and The Senior Major was David Hargreaves (subsequently, Colonel David). Company Commanders included Majors: Bernard Gordon-Lennox (Captain of the Queen's Company and subsequently Major-General Bernard, CB, MBE), David Fanshawe (subsequently, Colonel David, LVO, OBE), Christopher Airy (subsequently, Major-General Sir Christopher, KCVO, CBE) and Fritz Abel Smith. The Signals Officer was Captain George Alston-Roberts-West; Captain Charles Blackwood was the Transport Officer and Captain Oliver Lindsay (now Colonel Oliver, CBE) was the Intelligence Officer. The other officers included Lieutenants: John Baskervyle-Glegg (Reconnaissance platoon and subsequently Major-General John, MBE); the Honourable George Jeffreys; Paul Cordle; Alexander Heroys; Conway Seymour (currently, Regimental Adjutant); David Braddell; and Second Lieutenants Clive de Rougemont and Euan Houston (subsequently, SAS; currently Colonel Euan, OBE and President of the Grenadier Guards Association). (On our return to Wuppertal, Germany, David Gordon-Lennox joined the Battalion to take over from David Fanshawe, We were relieved by the 2nd Battalion, Grenadier Guards. I handed over to Captain Michael Hobbs (later, Major-General Sir Michael, KCVO, CBE) who was second Captain of number 2 Company of the 2nd Battalion. After a short time on Public Duties, based at Caterham, I returned to the Guards Depot at Pirbrght).

Chapter 22

"........NOT A TURK!"

Limmassol, Cyprus, Summer 1965

*I*n June1965, I had the great pleasure of being posted as the second captain of number 2 Company, under Major David ('shoot that bull') Fanshawe. He was one of the very finest of people and one of the most superb Regimental officers I ever met. In my humble opinion, had he taken the Staff College examination, he would have made an outstanding General, greatly to the benefit of the Army and of our country in general. Today, he still looks immaculately smart, as Colonel David, LVO OBE, in charge of Her Majesty's Body Guard of the Honourable Corps of Gentlemen at Arms. He made soldiering under any conditions both enormously satisfying and fun, for all ranks. The platoon Commanders were Lieutenant David Braddle and Second Lieutenant Euan Houston.

Lieutenants John Baskervyle-Glegg and Conway Seymour shared a room. Both young officers became extremely well suntanned. So deeply sunburned did they become, that their room was know as 'Turk Headquarters'. Conway, in particular, began to look like a caricature of a jovial and well-fed Turkish village *Mukta* or Mayor.

One of the duties of officers without platoons was to act as the Duty Officer on the battalion wireless net. We sat, with headsets and a logbook, in the Orderly Room. Most nights were very boring, with little or nothing to report. One night however, the quiet was broken by a most anxious radio transmission. . It ran something like this (These may be the wrong call-signs):

"Hullo 22. I am being held at gun point by a Greek Cypriot policemen." It was poor Conway Seymour in a high state of agitation. "What shall I do? Over," he added in a very concerned voice.

"Hullo 11 for 22. Just tell them that you're not a Turk. Over!" intervened John Baskervyle-Glegg.

"22. This is a *very* serious situation and that is *not* helpful. Out!"

Well, we were left only to imagine the apoplectic rage at call sign 22! The happy ending was that Conway survived without a scratch. Perhaps his impeccable command of the English language saved him, or even the smell of whisky in his water bottle that finally persuaded the Greek that Conway was definitely not Islamic! I understand that this was so convincing that no physical proof was called for!

Footnotes.

1. On 10th December 2004, at the funeral of the late Major-General John Baskervyle-Glegg, it was moving to see Conway Seymour, himself recovering from recent surgery, struggle to his feet from his wheelchair in order to pay his last respects to his old friend.

2. David Fanshawe was given the nick-name 'shoot that bull' as a result of an incident at Windsor in 1956, if I remember correctly. Apparently, he had just dismounted Castle Guard and had returned to Victoria barracks. The Adjutant had received a telephone call from the police saying that a farmer's bull had broken lose and was terrorizing people in Eton High street. They requested 'Aid to the civil power!' Once deployed, the adjutant, in a blue frock coat, stood in the High street and, pointing from his monocled eye, gave the memorable order to David Fanshawe, still dressed in scarlet tunic and service dress cap and armed with a .303 Lee Enfield rifle, "Shoot that bull, Fanshawe!" He did and made his name.

3. Another fun 1st Battalion story is one I did not witness. It was relayed to me by Academy Sergeant Major Ray Huggins, who was then (1946/7) a young Guardsman in the 1st Battalion that had just moved from Berlin to barracks in Nuemunster.

On Saturdays, the routine was Commanding Officer's parade, kit inspection and a cross-country run. Anyone missing the final note of the 'maximum time' bugle call, had to do the run again in the afternoon, accompanied by one of the Drill Sergeants, on a bicycle. They were fit in those days!

Sergeant-Major George Hackett (later Lieutenant-Colonel, MBE and now the most senior Quartermaster in The Regiment, prepared the parade. It was a misty winter Saturday morning. George Hackett gave out the then traditional words of command to the 700 or so men on parade (excluding many of headquarter company): "Sergeants in waiting!" They were then 'paced out', into precise locations by the Drill Sergeants. Following that, George Hackett called out, "Get-on...Parade!" Some 700 hundred immaculately turned out Grenadiers advanced, sloping arms as they stepped off and halted, with a single 'crack'. At that solemn moment, a very brave Guardsman, in the barrack block immediately behind the Sergeant Major yelled out of the window, "Get off again!" There was chaos in the midst as some men, who recognised an unauthenticated voice, stood fast whilst others, who did not, obeyed. There was an immediate 'cordon and search' of the barrack block. The brave Grenadier culprit lost his name so badly that it does not survive, to my knowledge. Indeed, he may well by now have lost a couple of inches in height! The search, however, yielded far more interesting booty. Besides a few skivers, some half dozen women were discovered in the loft, where they lived in apparent luxury, supported by the men in the barrack block. Clearly The Regiment had not forgotten the days of the American Revolution when it provided companies to act as Marines for the Royal Navy. This service earned the privilege of playing 'Rule Britannia' (a woman, of course!) at Tattoo. It was the custom in the Royal Navy in the days of the Almighty Horatio Nelson for women to be 'kept on board' ships of the line. Of course, they were justified as superb nurses, in case of war! Below decks, they were treated with respect, hence the reveille call, 'show a leg'. If a female leg appeared, the hammock was not turned-over.

Tradition dies hard in the Grenadier Regiment. In 1963, the 2nd Battalion took a recruiting team through the strong Grenadier country of Nottingham, Stoke-on-Trent, Derby, Worcester and Manchester. The team included Pipes and Drums, a company drill team, the Signals and Reconnaissance platoons and some PTI's. One night, we all slept in a massive baronial hall. The next morning, the Adjutant, Captain John Magnay, was disturbed at the slow pace of reveille. He stormed out of his sleeping bag and started 'spilling' men out of their sleeping bags. He then up-ended one, where a Guardsman fell out, but accompanied by a naked woman! It appears that tradition does indeed have its advantages and its stoic supporters. I feel that had it been used for recruiting, The Regiment would be the most over recruited regiment in the world!

Part Six

THE GUARDS DEPOT, PIRBRIGHT

The Guards Depot at Pirbright was very different from the old Guards Depot at Caterham. It was more modern and life was certainly more relaxed. However, the training has equipped the Household Division well for the types of limited war and internal security roles that our country has faced over the past 60 years. Whether or not this new type of training proves to be better than that of Caterham, in the trauma of a major strategic war, will have to await the judgment of history. I hope that day will remain far off.

When I was there, Pirbright was extremely well administered. Lieutenant Colonel David Scott-Barrett (Scots Guards) was the Commandant. The Second in Command was Major The Prince John Gikkar (Irish Guards) and the Adjutant, Captain Michael Hobbs (Grenadier Guards). The Sergeant Major was Tom Pugh (Grenadier Guards).

I took over, as Second Captain of 14 Company, from Captain Richard Micklethwait. (He had the heaven-sent medical condition that excused him all drills, but allowed him to hunt foxes. I tried hard, but in vain, to find it in a medical book, as template armour against further drills!) I served mainly under Major Nicholas Hales Pakenham Mahon and Major John Smiley. From memory, the Company officers included Lieutenants: Nigel Chancellor, Anthony Dennison-Smith and Nicholas Boggis-Rolfe. The Company Sergeant Majors were: Reg Page, BEM, and Jim Eastwood (subsequently, Major James, LVO, MBE, now, The Regimental Archivist). One legendary Gold Sergeant at that time was the late Sergeant Ray Barnes, who was later selected to replace Sergeant Major Ray Huggins as the Academy Sergeant Major at Sandurst. The Junior Guardsman's Company was commanded by the late Major Rags Courage CVO, MBE, a fine cricketer, he showed great humanity and good judgment. He was ably assisted by another Grenadier, Lieutenant Algy Heber-Percy, and by Lieutenants Johnny Morris (Scots Guards) and Graham Vere-Nichole (Welsh Guards).

The main advantages of Depot life, in my opinion, were getting to know more of the officers and non-commissioned officers in the other regiments of the Household Division. Also, life was more organised, with less impromptu time demands. On the other hand, Regimental Headquarters did use officers stationed at the Depot for some interesting short-term assignments. Pirbright was also near Windsor and the Guards Polo Club!

Chapter 23

A Man Called Churchill

State Funeral of Sir Winston Churchill, St Paul's Cathedral, 30th January 1965

On taking over the contents of a company safe in the Household Division most officers became familiar with a document in a purple hard cover with a black border. It was entitled 'State Funeral of the Right Hon. Mr. Winston Churchill'. The word 'Mr.' was subsequently scratched out in ink and written over it was the word "Sir". Legend has it that Sir Winston was unofficially offered a Dukedom after the Second World War. (It would have been the only non-royal Dukedom created in the 20th Century). Rumour has it that he declined the honour. Of course, it should be remembered that, as a young MP, he had campaigned actively for the abolition of the House of Lords. He was then offered a State Funeral (only the second to be offered to a Commoner, the other being given to the First Duke of Wellington). The funeral was based upon the format of the Great Duke's, Sir Winston requesting burial at Bladon churchyard, on the edge of Blenheim Park, near his Marlborough ancestral home of Blenheim Palace, and that 'Old Father Thames' be included in the proceedings. Apparently, the great bronze candlesticks, cast from captured French cannon for the State Funeral of Wellington, were used for only the second time at Sir Winston's ceremony.

A State Funeral is a very major event. By its nature it occurs irregularly and with little or no warning. Before computer storage, when old documents decayed, much of the organizational 'know how' became the stuff of personal 'folklore', stored in the heads of men of appropriate eminence, such as the Earl Marshal and

Garter King at Arms. On this occasion, Sir Winston's Private Secretary, Sir Anthony Montague Browne, assisted in putting the bones on a plan previously drafted by my former Commandant at Caterham, Colonel Vernon Erskine-Crum ISO (Scots Guards and subsequently, Lieutenant General Sir Vernon-the Imperial Service Order, was, even then, a rare medal, dating from the British Raj).

Obviously, any rehearsal before the actual death of the subject is likely to be a most delicate matter. Added to this, a State Funeral involves a great number of people. In this case, some 6,000 men and women from all the Services were to take part in a major ceremonial parade covering about a mile in size, with some complicated movements and timings. Many of them were unaccustomed either to ceremonial or to Guards drill. For example, the Royal Navy sailors who drew the Gun Carriage were used to slow marching not only to a different measure of pace, but also to a different timing of pace. Clearly a very great deal of planning, administration and practice needed to be carried out in the very short period of about a week. Finally, a State Funeral takes place in London, where modern traffic and road patterns have to be put to one side, even for rehearsals. Therefore time, as so often in war, is a key resource.

*I*n early January 1965 Sir Winston Churchill became ill. By January 18th his health had weakened considerably and the spectre of his imminent death was raised. Major General Sir John Nelson was commanding London District. He made a bold and timely decision to set in motion plans for the reconnaissance of the State Funeral, on a very discreet basis, by parade marshals. We were all briefed informally and assigned tasks. I was nominated, under Lieutenant Colonel Alan Breitmeyer, (Grenadier Guards and now a Brigadier) my former Senior Major, to be a 'Marshal' or Usher in charge of the Pall Bearers to The Coffin.

As Sir Winston wished to be buried in the actual soil of England, and not in a tomb, his coffin was lead-lined. Even after some metal stripping it weighed close to 600 pounds (a normal Royal coffin then weighing around 370).

Contrary to some stories, the Bearer Party was provided not by the Queen's Company, Grenadier Guards but by men of the 2nd Battalion, Grenadier Guards. Ironically, this was the very same battalion as that in which Sir Winston himself had served (attached) as a Major, in the trenches during the Great War. It was also the same battalion that was commanded by his ancestor John Churchill, Ist Duke of Marlborough, some 250 years beforehand.

I had just handed over the wonderful former (British Guiana) 'Star' Signal Platoon of the 2nd Battalion to Lieutenant Anthony Mather, who was assigned to be in charge of the Coffin Bearer Party. If I remember correctly, this included Company Sergeant Major Williams and two of my former signallers, Guardsmen Nick Wright and the late Guardsman Malcolm Surman. I understand that the Bearer Party started to rehearse, incognito. The rest of us were put on standby. Sir Winston Churchill's condition continued to worsen, but he held on like an old lion. The world waited for news bulletins from Hyde Park Gate.

On the afternoon of Saturday 23rd I was visiting a girl friend in a London art galley when the telephone rang. Ronald, the owner, handed me the telephone saying, " John, it must be for you."

'What?" I said before listening.

"Are you Captain Browne?" a mysterious voice enquired.

"Yes, I am."

"Then you will understand what I mean when I tell you to report to New Palace Yard tomorrow morning at 0930 hours?"

"Yes, I do understand."

"Good. Any questions?"

"No, thank you."

"Good, that's all. Goodbye."

Well, clearly, we had been moved to a higher state of readiness.

The next morning we were briefed in much more detail in New Palace Yard in the shadow of Big Ben's tower and allowed to 'walk the ground'. We then heard that Sir Winston Churchill had died about an hour and a half beforehand and that the Prime Minister had decided that his State Funeral would be the next Saturday, January 30th. Her Majesty The Queen was due on a State Visit to Ethiopia two days later. At Westminster Hall, during three days lying-in-state, some 300,000 filed slowly and silently past the coffin.

As Marshals to the Pall Bearers we were allocated the Armoury of Saint James's Palace as our Assembly Area and Saint Dunstan's Chapel, in Saint Paul's Cathedral, as our Forming Up Point. We were also given a fleet of some six Austin Princess motor cars, with wonderfully patriotic FANY drivers, to carry our Great Men, or 'charges'. Subsequently, we had some more, very specific briefing at Horse Guards by Colonel The Lord (Paul) Freyberg, OBE (Grenadier Guards) and by Major Simon Weber-Brown (formerly Scots Guards, and recalled from the City for the occasion because of his store of bespoke knowledge).

The Pall Bearers consisted of many of my schoolboy heroes. From memory they included: Admiral of the Fleet The Earl Mountbatten of Burma, RN; Field Marshal The Earl Alexander of Tunis (Irish Guards); Field Marshal The Viscount Slim; Field Marshal Sir Gerald Templer; General The Lord Hastings 'Pug' Ismay (Wartime Chief of Staff to Sir Winston who, apparently, used the Edwardian General to insulate himself from 'Intellectuals'!); Marshal of the Royal Air Force The Lord Portal; The Lord Normanbook; former Prime Minister, The Right Honorouble The Earl Clement Atlee (Deputy Prime Minister throughout World War Two); former Prime Minister, The Right Honourable The Earl of Avon (as Sir Anthony Eden, wartime Foreign Secretary); former Prime Minister, The Right Honourable Mr. Harold Macmillan (Grenadier Guards) and former Prime Minister, The Right Honourable Sir Robert Menzies, of Australia. It was a most impressive and historic group of leaders. It was my great honour and privilege both to meet and to administer to them over the next five days or so.

STATE FUNERAL of Sir Winston Churchill, 1965.
The Coffin arrives at St. Pauls. CSM Williams, followed by
(Signaler) Gdsm Surmon in Bearer Party .
Bottom left, Lord Avon, Field-Marshal Lord Alexander

CSM Williams leads the Coffin Bearers as the Pall Bearers offer their final salute to their old friend, 'The British Lion'.

Background Pall Bearers: Lord Alexander (L) and
Lord Mountbatten (R).
Foreground Pall Bearers: Mr. H. MacMillan (L)
and Sir R. Menzies (R).
Bottom right Lt-Col A. Breitmeyer.
Far left; Capt J.Browne, still holding Lord Slim's sword and belt.

One of our first tasks was to hand-deliver some of the official invitations to our Great Men. The one I remember best was the delivery to Lord Atlee in his apartment at Lincoln's Inn. He read the Letter of Invitation and initial instructions with quite amazing speed. Then he turned back from his desk and, with a look of defiance in his eyes, said "if [old] Ismay can do it, so can I!" (Ismay was two year's Atlee's senior). This remark was to prove the character of Lord Atlee and it contrasted vividly with the response of Field Marshal The Viscount Montgomery, who was recuperating in South Africa and is alleged to have replied, in declining the invitation, that he did 'not want the death of a friend to lead to his own death.' On a number of occasions over the next week, when we met with all the other Pall Bearers, I was impressed at how much all of them loved Atlee. Although very quiet and bent over with age, he was always in demand. There was an outpouring of genuine political warmth, not enjoyed by some others.

We had quite a workload over the next few days, the most dramatic of which were those of the rehearsals. The full rehearsals were carried out in the very early hours of the mornings, so as not to disrupt the London traffic, of Tuesday 26th and Thursday 28th of January. It was uniquely dramatic to see a skeleton formation of brigade strength of service men and women, led by some of the 'First of the Few' fighter pilots, with drum majors marching in State dress through the hushed and darkened streets of London to muffled base drums. To be in a quarter-lit, cold and near empty Cathedral and witness uniformed men quietly and ceremoniously bring in a coffin, was like witnessing the opening scene of a dramatic movie, depicting the important, but secret funeral of some great warrior leader.

At one stage in the proceedings the Pall Bearers, on a given word in a hymn, were required to turn westwards and start processing out of the Cathedral. One of the two key flank figures to trigger this movement was Sir Robert Menzies, former Prime Minister of Australia. Sadly, he was so moved and carried away that he kept missing his cue. His opposite number was Harold Macmillan who, as a Grenadier, was always on cue! The result was chaos. The Queen's Earl Marshal, Bernard, Duke of

Norfolk, who admirably managed the high occasion of State dressed in a magnificent fur-lined cloak, was not amused. When it happened he would shout out, "Stop! Stop! Stop!" pulling up the choir very sharp and bringing the music to an unmelodious and grinding halt. Striding impatiently up to Sir Robert, under the great, echoing Dome of Saint Paul's, he would shout, "I will not have it. You, Sir, must *concentrate*. The whole Service hinges upon you at this moment. You have a key role to play. Everyone depends upon *you*. You *must* concentrate, Please concentrate, Sir!"

Sir Robert, overcome with emotion and embarrassment, would murmur a heartfelt apology.

"All right. Again! Take it from the beginning of the same verse," the Duke would repeat before returning to his place with awesome dignity.

This happened several times. Each time the tension mounted. Sir Robert was almost in tears. It was sad, but also quite beautiful, for it showed the unmistakable wealth of affection Sir Robert, a declared Anglophile, had for his old wartime friend. It also illustrated, however, the great authority vested in the Earl Marshal of England. You have to be pretty senior before you can repeatedly give publicly shouted rockets to the former wartime Prime Minister of a most important Allied Nation. (Legend has it that, had anything happened to Sir Winston, Sir Robert Menzies would have been called upon to replace him as 'our' war leader.)

After a lot of truncated rehearsal and preparation the great day arrived and, using our fleet of limousines, we gathered the Great and the Good in our Assembly Area at Saint James's Palace. We needed to be in good time in order to help them with their kit. I remember two conversations, in particular. Field Marshal The Viscount Slim, who had risen from the rank of private soldier, noticed me surreptitiously admiring his Field Marshal's baton. He said, "Go on, John, take hold of it!" I hesitated and he added, " Go on, you have much more chance of getting one than I ever did!" I did as he instructed. I must say, it felt very grand, but I never quite earned one for myself but it was a rare moment to savour.

General 'Pug' Ismay lamented to me, "You know it's a pity

this is not a summer funeral."

"Why do you say that, Sir?"

"Because I am the only Edwardian General on parade and therefore the only one entitled to wear a scarlet tunic!" he said with a mischievous laugh. It showed how truly old and bold he was. He was the most charming of men. I could see why Sir Winston loved him.

At the allotted hour we 'climbed' aboard our fleet of limousines and led off towards Saint Paul's Cathedral. Thank God there was no need for map reading, for it was not a good time to get lost! The streets were fully lined with personnel from all three Services. The crowd was enormous and filled not just the pavements but most of the windows, balconies and even the rooftops along the line of route. Even the least sensitive of people could have felt the deep, heartfelt emotions of loss and of reverence. It was an experience of a lifetime.

We formed up, as planned, in Saint Dunstan's Chapel where we had prepared coffee for our Great Men. It was a very cold January day. I remember one of the Royal Heralds. He was dressed in his 'Royal Card' outfit and silk stockings. He was frozen and had approached me from the outside steps saying "I'm the oldest thing in the place and I'm frozen stiff." I smuggled him into our Chapel and gave him a cup of our hot coffee. He was so grateful. I felt as if I had given him vital water in a desert.

Just before we moved out onto parade we assembled at our 'Start Lines' close to the inside of the Great West door. We had superb and very close views of those arriving including HM The Queen, all the members of The Royal Family, President de Gaulle of France and President Lyndon Johnson of the United States.

As the main Procession approached to the solemn *Dead March of Saul* we moved, with our Great Men, out through the Great West door to our position at the bottom of the outside steps. The coffin arrived by Royal Naval gun carriage and was offloaded by the Grenadier Bearer Party. We preceded the coffin up the Great Steps and down the main aisle. Lord Atlee was weak. I had kept a special eye on him. As we climbed the Great Steps I saw him begin to struggle. I lent him my right arm. By the time we neared the top he was almost unconscious, but he fought on. Once we reached the main floor of the Cathedral he began to regain his composure. I watched very carefully to ensure he was better and stayed with him as far as I dared, without getting in the way. He survived the Service, which itself was nothing short of magnificent. With the name of 'John Browne' I have always had a soft spot for the 'The Battle Hymn of the Republic'. I must admit that my chest did swell just a little bit as I felt the notes vibrate on a State Occasion and resound throughout the great Cathedral caverns of Saint Paul's!

Sir Robert Menzies was right on cue on the day and the Pall Bearers preceded the Coffin westwards along the aisle, down the Great Steps to a position where they were to turn inwards to face the Coffin which would pass between them, so that they could bid their last farewells. My attention was focused upon Lord Atlee who made it, in quite good order, to the farewell position. However, as the Great Men turned inwards there was an ominous clatter of a sword hitting the pavement. (Normally this would indicate that an unfortunate officer has fainted.) I looked round to see that, as he had turned, Field Marshal Slim's sword belt had given out. His belt and sword had clattered to the ground. He was trying vainly to kick out of the entanglement, but his spurs held his belt fast around his boots, threatening his physical stability. I rushed up, as the Coffin approached and started to undo his sword belt. He was in a bit of a fluster. To calm him I said, " Thank God, I'm used to getting rabbits out of snares, Sir."

He mumbled quietly, "That *is* lucky. Thank you so much, John."

I kept his sword, belt and slings. I held them, together, with my own Marshal's baton in my left hand, while I saluted. Luckily my own sword was sheathed.

In a moment the Coffin was upon us, born by Grenadiers, and our Great Men offered their last salutes and bows to 'The Man of our Century.' It was all most moving. (I have some superb photographs of these moments, signed by Lord Atlee).

While the Coffin was being loaded onto the Naval Gun Carriage, I had to escort Field Marshal Alexander across the stationary procession to one of our limousines which, waiting in a side street, was to take him to HM Tower of London, where he would receive the Coffin as Her Majesty's Constable of The Tower. We did not have much time as I had to get back before the Procession started off again. As a true Guardsman, The Field Marshal remained cool, so cool that he said to me laughingly under his breath and referring to Lord Slim's Field Marshal's sword and broken sword belt, which I was still carrying, "You know, these Line Officers, they just can't keep their kit in good order!"

"Sir," I replied. (It has always amused me how the single Grenadier word, 'Sir' can mean so many different things, depending upon the situation, syntax and the tone in which it is uttered).

I managed to return to my main position before the State Procession moved off. We watched as the historic procession passed before us. It was an unforgettable sight. I maintained my eye on Lord Atlee throughout and noticed him weaken visibly. He needed support, like a chair, I thought. He was now so frail that I decided, against all Guards protocol, to break ranks. This was a serious decision on a State Occasion but I trusted that Colonel Alan Breitmeyer would support me. (In the event, he did indeed.) I rushed up the Great Steps to the astonishment of some, as The Royal Family were dispersing (talk about being 'caught short!'), past the heralds and Captain Simon Cooper (Life Guards) commanding the Household Cavalry's dismounted, step, guard. Once in the Cathedral, I removed my bearskin cap, grabbed a chair and took it to the ailing Atlee. He, too, was very grateful saying, "Oh, thank you, John. Just what I need."

We returned, in our fleet of limousines to Saint James's Palace down the processional route and prepared our Great Men for home. For a moment, the roar of a fly past of Lightning jet fighters of the Royal Air Force filled our ears as they flew up 'Old Father' Thames and away into the winter sky, So ended the Churchillian Age and one of the most memorable days of my life.

The Right Honourable, The Earl Atlee, in'The Chair'.
(Apparently this became Reuter's photograph of the year)

Photographs by Fox Photos

Chapter 24

Polo—A Right Royal Rocket

"Withot the spice of guilt, sin cannot be fully savored."
—Alexander Chase

Cowdray Park, Summer 1967

In my humble opinion, polo is the very greatest of games. It combines riding skill, striking at speed and ball sense with tactics similar to a cross between soccer and rugby. Played well, it offers the sensation of great speed and hard body contact. Like golf or cricket, the thrill of a good, well-timed shot keeps one returning to the game, no matter how low one's level of skill. Like golf it has a handicap system that allows the worst to play with the very best and so to enjoy matches way above one's station and to learn faster, from high standard practice. Horse quality and control is often more important than personal playing skills. It is a surprisingly tough game and like skiing, has an exotic international après life. Even as a golf nut, I feel that polo is truly the 'Sport of Kings' especially when King's and Princes play. I sometimes feel it to be a sort of modern day 'Jousting', with coloured helmets and shirts, taking the place of the personal Helmet Crests and the family Coats of Arms of old.

I first became involved in polo at the Guards Polo Club at Windsor, in 1958. I was very lucky to fall under the skilled and enormously kind eye of Major General Claude Pert. He was in Probin's Horse (Indian Army) and a former 9-goal player in the English team. He was a superb teacher. To me and I am sure to many others of that era, even the sound of his voice evoked strong images of polo, just as did the voices of BBC commentators Major Brian Johnston, MC (Grenadier Guards) and John Arlott (one of my constituents) for cricket lovers.

At Windsor, we enjoyed superb grounds and played in a number of representative teams including, for our Regiments, the Guards Depot and the Guards Polo Club. Some were lucky enough to play also for some high and medium goal private teams. Imagine how my heart raced when General Claude Pert informed me that I had been invited to play in HRH The Prince Phillip's low and medium goal Windsor Park teams. I played in these teams for about two years in the late 1960's. When HRH Prince Charles was down from Cambridge he also played in the team. The Queen watched her husband play on many occasions, even in practice chukkas. The après life was also exotic. Dancing with The Queen was one of the memorable thrills of my life – as it would be for any man. However, like all 'limelight' roles, there was a downside - the added pressure to win at polo and not to make too many mistakes.

Due to the speed, the rapidly changing tactical situation and the physical danger of the game, people tend to shout a little, and sometimes a lot. I remember playing for the Guards Polo Club in a tournament at Mr. Lucas' Woolmers Park, against Clare Lucas (now Clare Tomlinson), who was then a 0–goal player but went on to be, as a 5-goal player, the best woman player in the world. Unfortunately, the shouting had been so bad in our young team that Mr. Lucas refused to give us our 'Runners-Up' prizes!

Another example of shouted instructions was in 1967 when a newly joined young ensign, Evelyn Webb-Carter (Grenadier Guards and subsequently, Major General Sir Evelyn, KCVO, OBE) fell from his pony when playing in a match under the captaincy of the late Major Ronald Ferguson (Life Guards, and father of HRH the Duchess of York). If you fall off in polo, it is best to stay lying on the ground, for the safety rules demand that the game must stop. If however, you remain standing, the game carries on, with your team minus 25 per cent of its strength. Like a true Grenadier, Evelyn jumped straight up after his fall. His captain, Ronnie Fergusson, galloped past yelling, " Lie down, you bloody fool, lie down!" Evelyn dropped to the ground instantly, like a shot giraffe!

It is true that the Windsor Park team did have its own fair share of shouting and Prince Phillip showed great zeal for the game. I was sometimes asked what it was like being given so many Royal rockets. In actual fact, in some two seasons worth of matches, I had only one Royal rocket. I found Prince Philip to be a very fair and encouraging captain, who took great care of his team. Indeed, he has always shown the same style as Colonel of our Regiment.

he Windsor Park team had entered a medium, 12-goal tournament at Cowdray Park. Our line-up was: Peter Palumbo (now The Lord Palumbo, 2-goals handicap) playing at number 1, like a centre-forward (old style!) or modern striker in soccer; The Marquis of Waterford, Blues (4 goals) at 2, like an inside-forward; HRH The Prince Philip, Welsh Guards (5 goals) at 3, like a half-back, and me (1 goal) at Back. (Back is a similar position to the full back in rugby and sometimes just as lonely.) We had won through some preliminary rounds at Windsor and were now in the Quarter Finals at Cowdray Park.

At one stage in the match we were being attacked. Marked closely by the opposing number one, I managed, extremely luckily, to connect with a bouncing ball by means of a nearside backhander. However, I was not skilled enough to ensure that the ball went out to either the left or right side. In fact, the wooden ball went like a rocket, but straight back—smack into the fast oncoming chest of Prince Philip, who was galloping up behind and being ridden-off hard. It must have hurt like hell, but he said nothing.

In a later chukka the opposition hit a long ball towards our goal and past me. The classic play for a low-goal player like me was to wait for the opposition lead player in order to ride him out and prevent him from following up with a second shot. If possible, one tried simultaneously to 'back-hand' the ball to a flank, to set up a counter attack. On this occasion, however, the opposing number one player was way out of position and far, far behind. I was both unmarked and unchallenged. However, I was far enough away from the opposition that a weak backhand shot could be picked up easily by an unmarked, attacking player. I thought I had sufficient room, with time available to 'steer' the ball around, in a series of tangential taps, to face the enemy goal. However, this is a dangerous play. If one misses any of the series of tangential taps, your goal is left wide open. (It was a decision similar to that facing a rugby full back in deciding whether to kick or to run the ball). It is therefore a movement normally attempted only by good, high handicap players—not by the likes of me! However, I judged it worth the risk in the circumstances. As I was part way through this high-risk movement, Prince Philip galloped past, being ridden-off hard. As he passed me he yelled out, "Oh no, no! You silly fool, just back it!" Sadly, I was committed and had to carry on, right or wrong. The good Lord must have been with me, for I made it, much to everyone's surprise and relief, including my own. I passed the ball to Tyrone Waterford who took the ball up field and passed to Peter Palumbo, who scored. It was an important goal and the crowd erupted. However, Prince Philip rode up to the 'line-up' for the start of the next play shouting, "John, that was *your* goal, well played!" I felt relieved, thankful and proud, all at the same time. But even that was not the end of it.

Following the game, we went to the changing room. Once he had stripped off his shirt, Prince Philip called out, "John." He pointed to a huge, perfectly round, red bruise on his chest (clearly the result of the ball I had hit into him at a gallop). He added, with a smile, "And this was *yours* also!" Moments like that were intoxicating and one of the thrills of life, under a great captain in the sport of kings.

Chapter 25

"Silence That Horse, Immediately!"

In order to really enjoy a dog, one doesn't merely try to train him to be semi-human. The point of it is to open oneself to the possibility of becoming partly dog.

—Edward Hoagland

Horse Guards Parade, Summer 1967

Whilst serving at the Guards Depot, I was asked to stand-in for the Colonel of The Regiment (Major General Sir Allen Adair, Baronet, GCVO, CB, DSO, MC, JP, who commanded the Guards Armoured Division in the advance from Normandy into Germany in 1944/5). He was the most charming and delightful of men, but was unable to ride in the rehearsal for The Queen's Birthday Parade. I had to parade at Wellington barracks, dressed in a frock coat and ready to ride a charger in his place. Riding on parade, with stirrups long, in the military parade fashion and with only woollen blue overalls on a highly polished hard leather military saddle, puts one in a relatively insecure position, as mentioned, if anything goes wrong. However, it was a great honour. My pleasure was increased further when I found that the charger I was assigned to ride was none other than dear old 'Brutus'. He was the horse upon which I had enjoyed some wonderful days of foxhunting at Melton Mowbary. I greeted him fondly and like to think that he recognized me and had forgiven me for the great crash I had involved him in a few years earlier. He looked superb, tacked up in magnificent Grenadier State Saddlery, one of several sets, presented to The Regiment by Field Marshal, the 1st (Great) Duke of Wellington, in the early 1800's.

We formed up in the central courtyard of Buckingham Palace. We then set off, through the archway, across the forecourt to the Victoria Memorial, (the 'Birthday Cake'), where we joined the waiting Sovereign's Escort of the Household Cavalry. We then processed down the Mall behind the mounted bands of the Household Cavalry. The Mall was bedecked in flags. An enthusiastic crowed lined the route behind the patient 'street liners', provided by the Foot Guards. On a beautiful sunlit June morning it was more than magnificent. The superb pageantry, when viewed from a horse, was sensational. I only wish that more people could savour such an event. The fact that I was due to be playing polo that afternoon in Prince Philip's Windsor Park team made it all the more stimulating.

All went well and after the 'Inspection', we returned to our positions under the Horse Guards Arch. However, following the Inspection, when 'Brutus' had passed close to and probably scented some of the mares upon which the Household Cavalry were mounted, he began to get restless. 'Brutus' was officially a 'gelding', but may not have been fully cut. Anyhow, having possibly scented some mares, he began to exhibit some of the signs of a rampant stallion. He started to snort loudly. His belly swelled and he pawed the ground. High pitched, flirtatious answering whinnies echoed back across Horse Guards parade, from the Household Cavalry. It was all getting rather embarrassing, when a Blues staff officer, Captain Jeremy Smith–Bingham (a Sandhurst classmate and an Olympic rider himself) approached me on foot, but looking extremely serious. He said gruffly, "Will you silence that horse, immediately!" Well, that may have been a legitimate and intelligible order in the Household Cavalry. However, a foot guardsman, like me, had absolutely no idea whatsoever how to silence an excited half stallion that was greatly enjoying an amorous horse conversation with several well-groomed, beautifully dressed and shapely young mares. I was at a complete loss, but God smiled. A moment or two later, the senior Drum Major called out the order for the Massed Bands to 'Troop'. The all-pervading sound and dramatic introductory beat of the bass drum firstly interrupted and then drowned the whinnies. It also jolted 'Brutus'. Like a good Grenadier, he came to order immediately. I was saved not by the bell, but by the drum and a Grenadier drum, at that!

Footnote
Strangely enough, I had a similar experience on another so-called gelding in the early 1990's I had entered a very low-level dressage competition at Cholderton, on the borders of my Parliamentary Constituency. I was riding a gelding that I had always found to be somewhat lazy in the ring and hard to keep going. However, on arrival at the show ground, he suddenly became very much 'alive' as he sensed some new young mares. It was so bad that he continued to be very difficult as we performed out dressage test. One particular transition from a trot to a canter was executed as if he had been stung by a warble fly. We gained embarrassingly low marks, but the chief judge was good enough to add a kind personal note to our scorecard. 'Well sat!' she wrote. Sadly, however, it was not the sign of a good dressage test!

KAITEUR FALLS, British Guiana,
The largest single, vertical fall of water in the world.
(Almost three times the height of Niagra Falls)

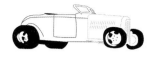

Chapter 26

"Which Regiment Are You In, Sir?"

A-4 roundabout, Hounslow 1960s (M3/M4, not yet completed)

After attending the wedding of a brother officer at the Guards Chapel in London, it was well past midnight when I left to return to The Guards Depot at Pirbright, still dressed in a morning tailcoat. These were the days before speed cameras and the police were not politicised and far more tolerant. I must admit, I had travelled somewhat fast down the almost deserted A-4. However, I was not overly concerned because I was in training and had drunk very little.

As I approached the Hounslow roundabout, I noticed that both the right and left hand lanes were occupied, but the centre lane was free. For many years, I had travelled this route to my family home in Wiltshire. Absent-mindedly, however, I had forgotten that this time I had to turn left for Pirbright, rather than go straight on for Bath. Impatient to make good time and get some sleep, I rashly thought I would out accelerate the motor car to my left and turn left in front of it. This was not only foolhardy, it was a bad decision, a very bad decision indeed. As the lights turned to green, I accelerated fast, but the motor car to my left accelerated far faster than I had expected it to do. I turned left aggressively in front of it, forcing it to stop against the curb. It was outrageous driving and very stupid. I was not proud but was keen to get on. In a second, I realized that I had been even more stupid than I had at first felt. The other motor car turned out to be a black police car! Its blue light flashed immediately and I pulled over, thinking I would be lucky even to be allowed to continue driving that morning let alone be saddled with a Court appearance and a serious fine with an adverse entry on my driving license. Worse yet, I was in a morning tailcoat and it was two o'clock in the morning. I was a perfect target for a police constable eager to climb the promotion ladder. It looked as if I was well and truly in the proverbial. I watched in trepidation, in my rear view mirror, as the police constable got out of his motor car and walked very slowly and deliberately towards me, whilst removing a notebook and pencil from a breast pocket.

"Good morning, Sir," said the constable in a voice straight out of a comedy show.

"Good morning, Officer," I replied meekly, thinking that a bit of promotion and flattery might ease my plight, just a wee bit.

"In a bit of a hurry are we, Sir? Do you realize that you almost forced a police car off the road, Sir?"

"I did not know it was a police car, Officer. I realize I acted stupidly, but I mistakenly got in the wrong lane, Officer."

"Yes, you do appear to have been in the wrong lane, don't you, Sir? Might I ask where exactly you were *hoping* to go to, Sir?" His emphasis on the word 'hoping' worried me more than a little.

"Pirbright, Officer."

"Oh, Pirbright! Really, and what may I ask will you be doing there, Sir?"

"I'm at the Guards Depot at Pirbright, Officer"

"And which regiment are you in, Sir?"

"I'm a Grenadier."

"Well that's very unfortunate for you, Sir, because *I* was a Coldstreamer," he growled, standing back and rising to his full height. My heart sank again. 'Those darned Lilywhites are 'something else', I thought. Allowing a moment or two for the gravity of my situation to sink in, he paused before bending down to address me again.

" You know you did very wrong, don't you, Sir?"

"Yes, of course I do, Officer, and I apologize."

"Well Sir, I was not only a Coldstreamer, I was a Guardsman. So, count yourself lucky and don't try racing a police car again. Is that clear, Sir?"

"Absolutely clear, Officer and again, I apologize."

" Carry on Sir, but drive more carefully in future. Next time, you may not be so lucky."

"Thank you Officer and Good night."

"Good *morning*, Sir!

Wow, what a stroke of luck! Who said there is no God up there? I drove off with great care and with a sense of both massive relief and of great thanks to all those fine souls who had created such a wonderful spirit of brotherhood in the Household Brigade.

Footnote:

My mother rather quaintly used to 'advise' me, "John, if you must speed, please do so sensibly!" Regretfully, with the introduction of speed cameras, this freedom is now denied.

Morgan Stanley,
New York 1971
Sales Platform.
(note: JP Morgan's
old roll top desks)

Morgan Stanley.
View from a window,
showing the
World Trade Center
under construction.
1971

Part Seven

CIVILIAN LIFE

The Greek teacher, Aristotle, said that to be properly qualified to be a politician one should first serve in the army for ten years and then undertake a further ten years in commerce. I did exactly that. Possibly I should have aimed off for the intervening 2,000 years, but I enjoyed my ten years with the Grenadier Colours enormously.

Due to a polo accident, whilst playing against a team captained by the Maharajah of Jaipur, I spent my last days of service in the army at King Edward VII's hospital. The Matron, the legendary Miss Saxby, saved my right knee from permanent injury and gave me many more years of mobility and wonderful sport. I will remain eternally grateful to her and to the wonderful visiting surgeon, whose name I have regretfully forgotten.

Upon leaving the army, I took a Master of Science degree at the Cranfield Institute of Technology. I was also lucky enough to scrape a place on the Master of Business Administration program at Harvard.

Bankers and Pashas, Saudi Arabia, 1974
Offering financial advise in the desert, or
was it falcon hunting?

Bankers and Swiss Gnomes, Switzerland.
Fun banking on the Cresta Run! (from Junction)

Chapter 27

A Royal Tribute to the Regiment

"But once a Grenadier, always a Grenadier."
—Winston Churchill, in a letter to a friend, 1920

The River Club, New York, September 1968

My Mother had a soft spot for the Duke of Windsor and I had been fascinated by his story. By strange coincidence, my Regimental dress sword (with 'EviiiR' engraved into the grenade on the hilt) was made for his Coronation, which never took place.

When passing through New York one of my American friends put me up in the River Club on the Upper East Side of Manhattan. It was a most comfortable club on the West bank of the East river. It offered me a prime location for making some acquaintance with New York City. The dining room had a superb mural of a nineteenth century naval battle between the Royal Navy and the new American Navy. Most unusually, the British lost on this occasion.

Having dined there one night, I sat down to have coffee in the drawing room. When I had finished I rose from my chair to leave for my room. To my great surprise, Their Royal Highnesses, The Duke and Duchess of Windsor sat down at the coffee table beside mine. By chance, I was wearing a Brigade tie. Clearly, it caught the attention of His Royal Highness. As I passed, he smiled and said, "Which regiment are you in?"

"I'm a Grenadier, Your Royal Highness, " I replied, recalling the old adage of 'Once a Grenadier, always a Grenadier' and bowing my head towards him and then smiling at the Duchess.

"Fine Regiment. I learned my soldiering in the Grenadiers before my appointment as Colonel of the Welsh Guards. They're the best of the best...Yes,... the best!" he added, nodding his head.

"Thank you, Sir," I replied.

"Are you still serving?" he asked, having clearly not quite noticed the length of my hair.

"No, Sir," I replied.

"What are you doing in New York?"

" I'm on my way to Harvard, Sir."

"That's a fine University. What are you reading?"

"I'm doing an MBA at the Business School, Sir."

"Tough stuff, I hear." Smiling, he then added, "But, good luck."

"Thank you very much, Sir," I replied, bowing my head again, before moving on.

As I left the room, I thought what a wonderful tribute to The Regiment, from a former King and Colonel-in Chief, who had served as a Grenadier, on the Western Front in the Great War. As a tribute, I felt it was fair, fantastic and fitting.

Footnote

I was reminded of a story told me by one of my signallers, Lance Sergeant Gerry Chamberlain. His Mother, Christine Chamberlain, had sent him a letter recalling a moment when she was working as a Care Giver in Hastings Hospital. One of her elderly patients started to talk to her about the First World War. He asked if her father had served in it. She replied that he had indeed, in the Grenadier Guards (see also Chapter 18, which points out that her future father-in-law in the Royal Artillery was unknowingly in direct support of her father on the Somme). Her patient's face lit up and he beamed adding, " I have all the regard in the world and the very greatest respect for the Grenadiers. One night, I joined my battalion as a battlefield replacement. I was a volunteer and only 17 years old. The next day a barrage started up and all hell let loose around us. I was terrified. Luckily, we had some attached Grenadiers in our trench. They took me in, calmed me down and generally looked after me. Ever since then, throughout all these years, I have regarded the Grenadier Guards with total respect. They were 'MEN'. I salute them to this day." Christine Chamberlain thought that her young Grenadier son would like to know of such a tribute to The Regiment.

Guards Polo Club, Windsor, 1967
H.M. The Queen presents Polo Cup
(Note: H.R.H., Prince Edward, as a young boy at fence
on far right)

Chapter 28

"Polo? Polo is the Last Thing We Need at this Time"

Harvard Yard, November 1968

Following the Second World War polo had been played at Harvard only on an ad hoc basis, when some players got together informally. There was no established polo club, as such.

Fresh from England and Smith's Lawn polo, I soon found some polo players and potential players. We decided to try to form a club. As always, financing was an acute problem. In America donations to academic institutions are tax-deductible. However the donations have to be for an 'activity' that is officially recognized at the institution. Polo was a casual and not an officially 'recognized' sport at Harvard. We had to get it accepted to have any chance of pulling in donations to our club. However, the late 1960s were the time of the SDS (Students for a Democratic Society), the Kent State killings and, a few weeks later, the Harvard strike. I attended the strike meeting in Harvard's Soldiers' Field stadium. The way in which the SDS abused and manipulated the democratic process would have made the British Trades Union leaders of the 1970s look like pink violets!

I was excited to be in America for the first time. I was lucky to be on the hallowed and beautiful campus of Harvard. It was thrilling in that, like the Grenadiers, 'quality' was a way of life. It was such a great privilege both to be taught by great professors (including Roland Christianson,

Miles Mace, Warren Law, Charlie Brown and Collier Crum) and to live amongst such fine and hardworking students (for instance, John Slocum, Emett Stephenson, John Williams, Valentine Nicholson, Jim Awad, Eddie Miller and Howie Cox). Especially in an institution that shared with The Regiment so many ideals, such as high standards, honesty, integrity and both self-respect and accountability for one's actions. The only striking difference was that the 'assault course' was more of an intellectual challenge than a physical one. Interestingly, 'sleep management' was a critically important factor. Colonel James Bowes-Lyon's advice to me, as a newly joined Ensign, about sleep management is also right on the mark in today's business world. We were over-faced with work by design, in the hope that we would learn to prioritise, the hard way. By coincidence, or design (?) the Harvard tie is identical to that of the Guards Division, save that the stripes go in the 'wrong' American direction! This must have led to some interesting confusion and near punch-ups in several English pubs! To this day, I try hard to concentrate on picking out the correct tie for our Black Sunday parade. It would not be good to be the only man in step on that occasion!

It was exhilarating at the Harvard 350th to see every major building decorated with three giant flags: the Crimson of Harvard, the Stars and Stripes of the United States of America and the Union Flag of Great Britain (sometimes wrongly referred to as the Royal Navy's Union 'Jack') commemorating its foundation and first 150 years or so of life, as an English university. Even the Commencement Speaker, HRH The Prince Charles (Welsh Guards) was in exactly the same college at Cambridge (Trinity) as was John Harvard, the Founder, some 360 years beforehand.

The diversity of people at Harvard was also both striking and impressive. In one finance class I remember marvelling at two particular people sitting next to each other. One was a slight man, Chan Daniels, leader and lead guitarist of the 'Highwaymen' group and arranger of such hit songs as *Michael row the boat ashore*'. The other was a very strong 'tank' of a man, Wilson Whineray, former captain of the New Zealand All

Blacks team and voted Rugby Player of the World for three successive years. Playing as coach in our rugby side, under the captaincy of Donald Nelson, he taught us all more about rugby than many of us knew existed and helped lead us to an unbeaten record. It is this great diversity and concentration upon standards that, in my humble opinion, provide the key similarities and strengths of both Harvard and The Regiment.

Having orientated myself, found a new apartment (more convenient to the campus than the one I had booked from England) and purchased the vast volumes of Case Studies and books containing 'required reading', my mind turned to sport. My first aim was to understand 'The Game',-American Football. I therefore booked a season ticket to Soldiers' Field. I was richly rewarded.

The year 1968 turned out to be the first time since 1906 that Harvard and Yale were both unbeaten and tied for the 'Ivy' League Crown in the last traditional game of the season. Although Yale, dressed in their 'Oxford' blue strip, were the very strong favourites, with three of their players (Calvin Hill, Ben Balme and Mike Pyle) soon to turn professional, it promised to be a great occasion and I took my fox hunting horn (the same one as in the parachuting, see Chapter 5) to help cheer for Harvard. In the event, the bulk of the game was uninspiring. As expected, Yale dominated. With only four minutes to go, they had 29 points on the board. Harvard, with one failed 'touch-down' conversion, had only 13 points. Yale had a lead of two converted touchdowns (6 points for a touchdown with an added 2 points for a 'touched down' conversion, as opposed to 1 point for the normal 'kicked' conversion). They both looked and felt quite certain of victory. On the far side of the stadium their band and crowd were already confident and tauntingly singing, "Yale's number one, Harvard's number two!" Worse still, mimicking the famous Harvard battle song, they sang out, "Ten thousand men of Harvard will *not* see Victory today!"

Then, suddenly, the Harvard coach decided to cast a last desperate dice. He substituted his Quarterback (a pivotal position, somewhat similar, in rugby, to a scrum-half). Within three minutes, Harvard scored a touchdown (six points) and executed a 'touchdown conversion, which many Yalie observers apparently failed to realise (another two points). The highest possible excitement pervaded the stadium. The score was now 29 to 21 with about one minute and forty seconds to go. Despite a valiant last minute effort, Harvard still appeared doomed. But, as so often in the affairs of sport, politics and war, the numbers sometimes fail completely to paint an accurate picture of human emotion and endeavour. This last touchdown, the antics of the crowd and a sense of great occasion somehow galvanized Harvard into overdrive. They appeared seized. It was that sudden change in morale, inspired by the illusive sensation we call 'hope'. Hope on the one side and fear, hesitation or even of relaxation on the other is often the stuff of legend in human affairs. Harvard kicked off, as in rugby. However, instead of a conventional long high kick, the kicker deliberately kicked the ball low along the mud covered ground. A large Yalie forward, unaccustomed to 'receiving', fumbled the slithering ball and Harvard regained possession from the kick-off a feat almost unheard of in American football. Now there were about 60 seconds to go on the digital stadium clock. Yale appeared rocked by the loss of certain re-possession. Against million to one odds Harvard scored yet again; just as the stadium clock went to 00.00! The game was over at 29 to 28, assuming Harvard converted successfully for one point, or so a significant number of the Yale crowd appeared to think as they swarmed across the field, singing and shouting, to taunt the Harvard team and crowd.

However, under Ivy League rules, the side scoring a touchdown can elect to forego a 'kicked' conversion attempt (for one point) and try to make another, single shot 'touchdown' converson play from a 'line' (or scrum) from the same position, but for two points. The Harvard coach had no difficulty in deciding to go for the latter. The excitement must have been like that when England won the rugby World Cup in 2003. The air was electric as the bemused Yale crowd was cleared from a third of the field to allow this single attempt.

The Harvard quarterback called the play and raced from

side to side of the field, narrowly squirming away from desperate, grasping, but menacing Yalie hands. (The film record is fantastic). I was so excited. I could not even sound my hunting horn. Then, after what seemed like an eternity, the quarterback saw an unmarked Harvard man and fired a rocket-like pass. It was held high and so was Harvard's honour. It was perhaps the most exciting five minutes in the history of American football. Legend was made.

That night, all the Harvard clubs and many of the bars around Harvard Square threw open their doors with drinks on the house. The next issue of the Crimson newspaper boasted the massive and historic headline, ***"HARVARD BEATS YALE, 29—29!"***

In the celebrations I met up with my polo friend, the late Adam Winthrop (formerly US Marine Corps and a former Harvard ice hockey and polo player. His ancestor had given John Harvard his library as the vital element in the foundation of Harvard, some 350 years before.) Adam had brought his youngest brother Jonathan (now a first class shot and an acclaimed architect) to see what became known as *The* game. We retired to the Porcelain Club, where I told him of our ideas to form an official polo club at Harvard. He was excited and approved wholeheartedly of a plan to approach the President of Harvard to ask that polo be made an 'approved' sport. He kindly offered to try to get us an interview with Harvard's President, Nathan Pusey.

A few days later we had our meeting with President Nathan Pusey. We asked that polo be recognized as an approved sport. President Pusey exploded, "Polo? Polo, is the last thing we need at this time, at Harvard!" Despite our pleadings, he would not be moved. We left downhearted, but not defeated. Polo has powerful friends, worldwide, we felt.

Thanks to the handicap system in polo one gets to play, especially practice chukkas, with players of a skill level way above one's station. I had the pleasure of meeting a Texas oilman before I left for America. His name was 'Hap' Sharp. He had brought a high-goal team to England the previous summer. We approached him. He was going to Argentina that winter to play and get more top class ponies. He was kind enough to present us with six of his 'trade-out' ponies.

In a matter of days we were back in President Pusey's office, this time armed with the telegram from Hap Sharp. President Pusey read it apprehensively. It read, words to the effect, 'so glad to hear you are starting regular polo at Harvard for the first time since the war, please arrange for sufficient transport to meet six ponies at Boston South station at such and such a date and time'. We added that, these ponies belonged not to us, but to Harvard. President Pusey was convinced and polo was recognized as an 'official' sport.

Financial and moral support flowed in to our new polo club, particularly from the polo fraternity in Myopia, who were most generous with money, time, training and even summer holiday stabling at the Myopia home of Crocker Snow, Junior (also a former Harvard ice hockey and polo player, together with Adam Winthrop. Subsequently he became founder and the Managing Editor of the American newspaper *World Times*). Crocker Snow was an accomplished 3-goal polo player and a correspondent for the *Boston Globe.*

In later years Crocker was invited to play, with Adam Winthrop, in a British army polo tournament in Berlin. To justify his trip for his temporary assignment sponsor, *Die Deutsch Wielde* (Radio), he interviewed, live, the Berlin Garrison Commander, Major General Sir John Nelson (Grenadier Guards). A keen polo player himself, General Sir John had organized the polo tournament, despite great international difficulties. For example, the German polo ponies had to be sold (temporarily) to the British before the Russians would permit them to be transported by train from the British Zone of Germany, through the Russian Zone, to the British Sector of Berlin. It was a most successful tournament, with Crocker on the winning team. The fact that such a tournament could take place at all had a good and, in those days, importantly positive political effect upon civilian morale in Berlin. Despite their overwhelming military strength, there were certain things the Russians could not control and it was important to highlight them.

Some people are tempted to scoff at the role of sport in political/military situations. However, one has only to remember that, in 1415, it was 'real' or 'royal' tennis balls that provoked England's greatest ever land victory, at Agincourt, in which King Henry V won the throne of France. One is left merely to wonder if he had not been so kind to his future father-in-law, in letting him off the hook over the French throne, whether we would have lost the American colonies, in the late eighteenth century! In the early 1970s, ping-pong played a key role in 'unlocking' Communist China. So, why not use polo to deride and chip away at the Communist tyranny in the late 1970's?

As expected between polo players, the Nelson-Snow recorded wireless interview went very well, until young Crocker was tempted to ask a decidedly cheeky, but media sensational, question as to how the front line of the British army could justify the use of British taxpayers' money and energy on having polo ponies along side their tanks in Berlin. Understandably General Sir John, still dressed in his Grenadier boating jacket, brown boots and white breeches, became apoplectic and the interview ended abruptly.

Subsequently, Adam Winthrop, Crocker Snow and I played in an 'Old Harvard' polo team with Russell Clarke, Senior and enjoyed much laughter, re-enacting this incident. I was invariably cast in the role of General Sir John. I must admit I did rather enjoy giving Crocker Snow a good Grenadier dressing down for many years to come. After he died, I often felt I could just hear the great General Sir John looking down upon us and saying, "Hear, hear, well said that man," as I repeated his strong words of anger and 'Foxtrot Oscar ' advice as to where young Crocker Snow should go. I have to admit that I still do get a certain kick out of it!

Anyway, regular polo was thus restored at Harvard. Our

first match, on February 8th 1969, was against Yale in the superb facilities given to them by the Phipps family. We lost, but regular polo was alive at Harvard. The first match against Oxford was played at Myopia (the Winthrop and Snow home ground), north-east of Boston, in the early 1980's.

Chapter 29

Morgan Stanley Have No Problem
with the Alphabet

Wall Street, New York, 1971

This story has no direct contact with the Grenadier Guards. However, Morgan Stanley was the only commercial firm I have seen that truly thrived by adopting Grenadier standards. Indeed, they were a thrilling testimony that Grenadier standards can be used by a commercial enterprise and result in outstanding financial success. It is for this reason that this story is included.

As a result of the Glass Steagle Act of 1934 the American Government forbade banks both to lend money and to underwrite the issue of Securities. In other words, Merchant banks were made illegal. Banks had to choose whether they wished to continue in operation as a lending, Commercial bank or as an underwriting, Investment bank. J.P. Morgan, son of the founder, Pierpoint Morgan, chose to remain exclusively a Commercial bank, based at 23 Wall Street. However, his eldest son, Henry, ran the Bond underwriting department at J.P. Morgan. He had all the skills and the clients of a great business. He and his partner, Stanley, therefore set up their own Investment banking firm, just up the street at 2 Wall Street.

Whilst at Harvard Business School I was recruited to join Morgan Stanley by John Young, the legendary managing partner and an associate, Richard Fisher, a man who was, in later years, to lead Morgan Stanley to even greater heights and to become one of the great titans of Wall Street. In terms of salary, Morgan offered less than any other major investment bank, but they were the best.

Morgan Stanley recruited exclusively from Harvard. Strict ethics, high quality business and total professionalism were the watchwords of their activity. The best and zero defects were required at all times. Everything that left the office was triple-checked. A lack of integrity or discretion was the surefire way to instant dismissal. They also combined the old and the new in a delightfully seamless manner. They were very traditional, insisting upon their own private typestyle and on having the sailing times of the great liners posted in the Partners' dining room. Extremely conscious of their name and prestige they would not agree to appear on any financial advertisement, except as the lead underwriter. If they participated in a syndicate, other than in a lead role, they asked that their name not appear in the so-called 'tombstone ' advertisement. On the other hand they were very modern. They were the first bank on Wall Street to give their staff a computer to use as a calculator. All of us were trained not only to use the computer, but also to write simple programs in Fortran IV. (Today, it is like looking back to the steam age, but in those days, it was ultra modern). Does that combination of the best of the 'old' with the best of the 'new' sound like The Regiment? It certainly did to me.

What was most thrilling was that Morgan Stanley was extremely profitable, retaining as clients many major governments and seven of the 10 largest companies in the world. To see Grenadier principles operate so well in commerce was inspiring and, in my view, worthy of note for Grenadiers, particularly young Grenadiers.

One day in 1971, Morgan Stanley won a new, major client, S.S. Kresge. As part of the welcome, the top management of Kresge was entertained to luncheon by Henry Morgan, in the Partners' dining room. At first they were shocked that Morgan Stanley served no alcohol at luncheon. (Unless you had an English guest, when one glass of sherry was permitted). After a sumptuous luncheon Henry Morgan gave a brief welcoming speech and invited questions. To everyone's surprise, a relatively junior member of the Kresge team asked a question. All eyes turned down the vast table as he spoke somewhat cheekily and sarcastically, "Tell me, Mr. Morgan, why does Morgan Stanley have such trouble with the alphabet?" Clearly, he was referring to Morgan's unique habit of appearing only first (like the First Guards?) or not at all in any financial advertisement. A hush fell over the room. The seniors of Kresge were mortified at their colleague's embarrassing lack of tact. All waited anxiously to see how the old Wall Street titan, Henry Morgan, would reply after such tactless provocation.

"Morgan Stanley," he said with a most charming smile and looking around the table, "have absolutely no problem with the alphabet...so long...so long as it begins with 'M'!" In great relief, all applauded and the day was saved.

Chapter 30

"Turn Out the Guard!"

Hong Kong, 1970's

In the mid 1970's I was the Director, Middle East operations, of a London- based merchant bank. My areas of responsibility included Project Financing, Lending, Bond Placement and Money Management. The Middle East had exploded with a level of liquid wealth unprecedented in history. The work was both exciting and interesting, but it required a very great amount of international travel. Everyone suddenly focused great attention on the Middle East and wanted to know both about the area and especially how to conduct local business. This resulted in yet further 'consulting' travel to other areas, such as the Far East.

W̱hilst on an extensive consulting tour of the Far East I visited Hong Kong. I was entertained by an old friend, Sir Lawrence Kadoorie CBE (later, The Lord Kadoorie) and his charming wife, Muriel, at their splendid 'country' home at eleven-mile point in Kowloon. Lawrence Kadoorie was one of the great Taipans of the Far East. His knowledge was prodigious and his advice was sought from all over the world. He was Chairman of Hong Kong Power and Light and had rendered wonderful service both to Hong Kong and to Britain during and after the War.

After luncheon, Lawrence insisted upon showing me around his new power station. He then invited me back for dinner. In declining his kind invitation I mentioned that I had been invited to dine with my old Sandhurst friend, Major Henry Hanning, who was currently serving with the 2nd Battalion Grenadier Guards in Hong Kong. He replied, "Well, we must send you over in an appropriate, Grenadier motorcar!" With that, he summoned his chauffeur to have me taken...in a Rolls-Royce!

At the barrack gate the Grenadier sentry's keen eye spotted a very stately green Rolls-Royce approaching. He must have thought the Governor was approaching to dine with the Commanding Officer (Lieutenant-Colonel Dermot Blundell-Hollinshead-Blundell, now a Brigadier. He had, I believe, just taken over from Lieutenant-Colonel David Fanshawe). Whatever it was, the Sergeant of the Guard clearly agreed and the Guard was duly Turned Out and brought to the 'Present'. I did not know the exact location of Henry Hanning's quarter, but I could not possibly stop the car and ruin the whole superb performance, so I told the chauffeur to 'drive on' and gave a 'royal wave' in acknowledgement. Once we were out of sight of the guardroom I stopped to ask some astonished Guardsmen for directions to Henry Hanning's quarter. It was not easy to find and I had to stop several times. Each time the helpful Guardsmen were clearly amazed to find a chauffeured Rolls-Royce being driven around barracks, but looking decidedly lost.

A superbly hospitable Elizabeth Hanning gave us dinner. Having enjoyed the spectacular view from her house over port, I summoned my fine carriage. I was fully expecting to have to acknowledge another smart 'present' by the guard. However, the Sergeant of the Guard was not going to be fooled again. This time, he saluted, but gave me a decidedly sullen look as I passed through the gate on my way out. It all goes to show that riding in a Rolls-Royce is more than merely driving in a motor car – it's an experience!

Chapter 31

Grenadier Teamwork at All Times

A tribute to The Earl of Lichfield

I was saddened to learn recently of the sudden death of Patrick, Earl of Lichfield. We first met at Sandhurst, when he was Lord Anson. All agree that he was one of the finest photographers of his generation. He showed a sure talent early on, when he was in The Regiment. In one of the Regimental scrapbooks, there is a photograph entitled, 'Hail Shinning Morn'. It is of Major Nicholas Hales Packenham Mahon (formerly Guards Parachute Company) in a suitable senior 'supervisory' pose on the rifle ranges, relying heavily upon his young platoon commanders, including Patrick, to 'carry on'!

When I think of Patrick, I think—'Grenadier teamwork'.

The first instance was at Sandhurst, where we had a number of collaborative transportation visits to London after dark. He was a very fast driver. I understand that later he and (Little/Nicholas Villiers established the record from Hyde Park corner to the 1st Battalion's Kandaha barracks at Tidworth (unlikely to be broken in these days of speed cameras). On one occasion, in the summer of 1959, several of the Grenadier Cadets, at Sandhurst were invited to dine with the officers of the 1st Battalion at the old Chelsea barracks. Realizing that this could be a very 'heavy' night, I took the precaution of driving my own motor car. If my memory serves, I think it was the Adjutant, Bernard Gordon-

Lennox, who wisely took the rotor-arm from Patrick's sports car. He came back with me and it was quite an event filled journey, especially getting back into Sandhurst.

The next evidence I saw of Patrick's ability to inspire teamwork was when he married Leonora, elder daughter of the late 5th Duke of Westminster. As one can imagine, it was a pretty grand affair held at Chester Cathedral, with the reception at Eaton Hall. Patrick was a cousin of HM The Queen, so a number of the Royal Family attended, including The Queen and The Queen Mother. We all stood as the bride arrived at the great door, on her father's arm. Patrick and his kinsman and Best Man, Brian Alexander (Irish Guards), were of course in the front row on the South side. Immediately in front of them stood HM The Queen in the choir, facing North. As we rose, the effects of Patrick's bachelor's party kicked-in dramatically: the Best Man fell forward in a dead faint, dropping the Ring. The Queen, like a true Grenadier, looked steadfastly to her front without a tremor. Meanwhile, a major Grenadier cooperation exercise took place amongst the ushers. First the Best Man had to be picked up and revived. Then the Ring had to be located and retrieved. Amazingly this was all accomplished by the time the bride arrived at the Communion steps to be greeted with calm smiles from, The Queen, Patrick and his ashen-faced Best Man. Fortunately the late Duke of Westminster moved slowly, being of a certain age, and Chester Cathedral has a long aisle!

Finally, some years later, in the days of the Shah's reign (mid 1970s) I was returning from a merchant-banking trip to Teheran. We stopped in Bahrain, where Patrick and his camera crew joined the flight. Evidently he had been on a picture shoot in the Middle East. *En route* to London, we had a grand time noshing back the champers and laughing about escapades, Grenadier characters and times past.

However, after an hour or two of flying, one of the other passengers became offensively drunk and disorderly. He caused great upset to the air stewardesses and to some of the other passengers.

Part of Patrick's camera kit included duck tape. Inebriated fellows can exert considerable strength, but, fortunately, only in a somewhat slow and uncoordinated manner. Anyway, with the help of Patrick's camera crew and a male steward, the offender was subdued and his legs, arms and chest taped to the seat. Under a threat to tape his mouth shut he quietened down, but he looked a right sight. The remainder of the flight went well or should I say even better! When we finally reached Heathrow, the police came on board, cut the detainee loose and, as they say, 'took him away'.

Patrick, whose kinsman was the fourth Colonel of the Regiment (1688), was a fine Grenadier. He was also a most entertaining friend, possessed of those two attributes, difficult to describe but instantly recognisable, of style and charm. We shall surely miss him.

Visiting Herr Strauss in Bavaria
Sir John Biggs-Davidson MP (Royal Marines)
and Rt. Hon Julian Amery MP (SOE)

JB with an 'ear being bent' on fast commuter train in
Winchester Constuency!

Part Eight

MEMBER OF PARLIAMENT

For me, it was a very great thrill to be elected to the House of Commons. My Party sponsors were General Sir Rodney Moore (Grenadier Guards) and Major Sir Henry Legge-Bourke MP (Blues, and Chairman of the Conservative 1922 Committee). Ironically, both their eldest sons, Michael and William, were in the Caterham Brigade Squad with me. I was especially privileged to represent the wonderful and historic constituency of Winchester. I rented a charming mini schloss at Rotherfield Park from my Lord Lieutenant, Lieutenant-Colonel Sir James Scott, Baronet. It was idyllic and also proved excellent from a security point of view. The police were pleased that both the Lord Lieutenant and the local MP were all under a single security watch and detail. I kept my horses at Rotherfield and much enjoyed riding with Jim at weekends over his beautiful estate. Although Hampshire is largely Greenjacket territory, I found myself surrounded by some fine Grenadiers, most of whom lived less than five miles distant. They included General Sir David Frazer,GCB,OBE; Sir Hugh Smiley, Baronet JP; Brigadier Peter Prescott, MC, Major-General Bernard Gordon-Lennox CB; MBE; Major 'Dicky' Birch-Reynardson; Captain

173

Damon De Laslo and CSM Ray Page, BEM. Jim's wonderful and spiritual wife, Anne radiated goodness and made Rotherfield a veritable home for the oppressed and for charity. Even the flowers appeared to bloom better under the gentle guidance of her gardener, aptly named Mr. Nettle. She also catered for some fine home shoots and these included further Grenadier guests, amongst whom I remember in particular Brigadier Anthony Heywood, CBE, LVO, MC and Lieutenant-Colonel Richard Heywood-Lonsdale MBE, MC, ERD.

As Winchester's representative in Parliament it was a great thrill to participate actively in perhaps the most fundamentally positive political revolution of our times: the Thatcher Revolution. Looking back, it was a truly great revolution. It can be summed up in a single word - Freedom. When we came into power, in June 1979, the top rate of income tax stood at 92 per cent. Foreign exchange controls allowed spending abroad of only 250 pounds Sterling a year, of after-tax money by each individual. We were not even allowed to own a telephone.-We had to rent it, exclusively from the Government monopoly telephone company. Trades Unions held undue sway and economically our Country was giggling its way into the ocean. The Cold War was still very cold (with the deployment of ground based Cruise missiles and the Presidential 'Evil Empire' speech), before the Great Thatcher/ Regan/ Gorbachev 'thaw'. I think people too easily forget just what the Thatcher Revolution achieved, politically, socially and economically and how much of the recent economic success Britain still owes to her. Margaret Thatcher was a truly inspiring leader and it was both a privilege and a very great thrill to serve under her 'Nelsonic' command. When I was a Cadet at Sandhurst, in the Summer of 1959, I remember visiting the House of Lords, as part of some course. I witnessed the first maiden speech of a women Member of the House of Peers. Exactly twenty years later, in the Summer of 1979, it was an added thrill to be a Member of the House of Commons and to sit listening to the first speech by a woman Prime Minister. In her speech she made emotional, special and most reverent reference to a very gallant gentleman whom I had met. His name was Airey Neave (Grenadier Guards) a famous graduate of Colditz prison camp and one of the the architects of Margaret Thatcher's historic battle to lead the Conservative Party. He had been murdered by the IRA, at the House of Commons, only weeks beforehand.

Before entering Parliament I served as the Councillor for Knightsbridge on the Westminster City Council. Added to the normal interests we had many State events. On ceremonial occasions at the Palaces, we were constantly under the able 'care' of such wonderful Grenadiers as Lieutenant-Colonel Sir Eric Penn, GCVO, OBE, MC and Lieutenant-Colonel Sir John Johnstone, GCVO, MC, both from Buckingham Palace. This ensured that, even as a ragged bunch of City Councillors, we measured up to the drill and form of State functions!

Rotherfield Park

Chapter 32

"Would A Peerage Be Enough?"

House of Commons, London, 1980

I was appointed to the Committee on the Industrial Relations Bill, introduced by The Right Honourable James Prior (Now The Lord Prior). It was a most important bill that formed a basic pillar in the 'Thatcher Revolution'. It laid the foundation for the curbing of the abuse of power by the British Trades Unions which had recently culminated in the 'Winter of Discontent' in 1979. However, I, and a number of my Thatcherite-Conservative backbench colleagues, felt that the Bill did not go nearly far enough in certain key areas. In particular, we felt that Trades Unions should hold a secret, democratic ballot of their members before they undertook industrial action. I knew from my mailbag and from meeting with delegations that many, perhaps even a majority of Trades Union members, agreed strongly with this point. Even the veteran Trades Unionist, The Lord ('Mannie') Shinwell told me that he supported the ammendment wholeheartedly, After all, it was democracy. Sadly, Jim Prior felt that our view was too aggressive and went too far, too fast. After many meetings with him, he refused to accept our point of view. We therefore tabled an Amendment to the Bill, for consideration at Report stage, by the full House. We then set about mustering support for our Amendment. I also tabled an Early Day Motion, which gained the strong support of over 100 Members, including some senior Liberals. Sadly, despite yet more meetings, Jim Prior would not give in, so we pressed on.

After one lobbying meeting with the Prime Minister in the House I came out of her office and into her waiting room. Assembled there were some very powerful Peers, almost all Grenadiers. From memory, they included: Major-General The Duke of Norfolk (Earl Marshal of England); Colonel The Right Honourable, The Viscount de L'isle VC; Lieutenant-Colonel The Right Honourable, The Earl of Cromer (formerly Governor of the Bank of England and HM's Ambassador to the United States of America); Major The Right Honourable, The Lord Carrington (Foreign Secretary); The Marquis of Salisbury and the Earl of Kimberly. I did not ask at the time but I was told later that they were also lobbying for our Amendment. With support like that we moved on with more conviction.

As luck would have it, our Amendment was 'selected' for debate. I 'led' at the Report stage. It was, to all intents and purposes, the first backbench rebellion against the Thatcher administration. Conservative discipline was very strict. Normally Margaret Thatcher would have one up on her 'Memoranda' even for abstaining from a Vote, let alone opposing her in one. The whole affair caused a small media frenzy. It gave me my first exposure of the massive power and pressure of the media. Even though the media supported me in a way, it was both awe-inspiring and worrying, from a democratic point of view. Later in my Parliamentary life I was to learn how totally overwhelming and brutal it can be if the media disagree with you.

On the day of battle the chamber was packed for the Third Reading (in days of old Bills were always read out in entirety by the Clerk of both Houses of Parliament, because many Members could not read). Our Amendment had become a major political talking point and also a major embarrassment to the Government. The Conservative Whips were extremely angry and had already subjected me to some of the fearsome 'third degree', at which they are notorious masters. When they threaten your Parliamentary career, you are made vividly aware that you are facing no empty threat. There are no warning shots - they shoot only to kill.

I introduced our Amendment to a tense and packed House. It was an awe-inspiring experience for a new Member. Grenadier training for 'steadiness under fire' came in very useful. There followed a keen debate. I can well remember my wonderful Parliamentary 'pair', the veteran Socialist, Ian Mikado (about whom Winston Churchill is said to have commented, "Mikado? He's as ugly as he looks!"). In his speech he ridiculed my shallow experience of industrial relations with words to the effect that, 'Mr. Speaker, the Honourable Member for Winchester has of course such vast experience of industrial affairs. I can see him now, Mr. Speaker, as he drives sedately through his constituency, looking up at the sky; a sky coloured red with the glow of all the fires in the steel furnaces below, stretching from Winchester to the sea!' It was all good fun from a formidable debater and a legendary Parliamentarian.

As the debate drew to a close around 9.50 pm, the House was again packed, including the Press Gallery. There was high tension in the air. As the Proposer I had the right of reply at the end of the debate. The Chief Whip, the Right Honourable Michael Jopling (now, The Lord Jopling) turned round in his seat near the Prime Minister and lent over to speak with me. He very kindly advised me to stand after the current speaker (the Minister) had finished and to make my speech short and to ensure that I sat down *before* ten o'clock. As I was leading the rebels I have to say that I admired his integrity in giving me helpful advice. I gave my short speech and the Vote was called. I put in 'Tellers' to force a Division. The Government had to Vote with the Socialists to defeat us, but we had over a hundred Conservative supporters, and some Liberals, in the 'Aye' lobby.

After the Division I gave a small press conference. Brian Shallcross, Lobby Correspondent of Southern Television, asked me, "What did the Chief Whip say to you?"

"Just some friendly procedural advice. Why do you ask?"

"Oh, the betting in the Press Gallery was that the Chief Whip, in seeking to kill your amendment, asked you, 'Would a peerage be enough'!"

For the next few days I waited apprehensively for a summons to the Prime Minister's memorandum at Number

Ten, but no notice-slip came. However, a few weeks later, I was summoned to her office in the House by my old friend, Ian Gow MP (15th/19th Hussars and, as *Private Eye's* 'super-grass', Parliamentary Private Secretary to the Prime Minister. Later he was brutally murdered by the IRA in front of his family). Hastily stuffing the proverbial blotting paper into the seat of my pants, I hurried off to face the 'Green Door' of the Prime Minister's office. She discussed the Bill briefly and intimated her plans in that area. It was clear to me that she not only approved of my amendment, but also intended to enact it in the next Parliament. I got the feeling that, given the political circumstances of that time, she had opposed it merely to support her ministerial colleague (Jim Prior). In the event, she did introduce the promised legislation. It is now law and I hope and trust that it has done much to improve the competitiveness of our country in world markets. However, it goes without saying that she did not recommend me for a peerage!

Chapter 33

"John, Do You Call This Boring?"

House of Commons, London, mid-1980's

A normal, non-election, Parliamentary year ends in early November, after the Party conference season and a brief tidying-up period for unfinished legislation in October.

Following Prime Minister's Questions at 3.30 pm on a November Thursday in the mid-1980s, Members bade each other 'farewell'. They prepared for a few days holiday before the State Opening of Parliament and the week-long series of debates on the Government's strategy for the coming year, as outlined in the Queen's Speech from the throne of the House of Lords.

A close American friend of mine was in London briefly. I took him to see the Guard Mounting at Buckingham Palace. He asked if there was any possibility that he could see "Margaret Thatcher at the Dispatch Box hitting the opposition for six!" Unfortunately, I was already engaged for luncheon and had given my Question Time tickets to a couple of constituents. I checked my schedule and invited him for dinner, with the *caveat* that, following Prime Minister's Questions, almost all Members of Parliament would depart, leaving the House almost deserted as a minor debate wound up the final hours of the Parliamentary Session. Still excited, he accepted.

We had a drink in the Strangers' Bar and sat down to dine in the near-deserted Strangers' Dining Room at about 8.45 pm.

We enjoyed a good dinner, with much Harvard nostalgia and discussion of Westminster politics and the achievements of the 'Blessed Margaret.'

At about 9.35 pm my guest noticed the words 'Rt. Hon. Michael Heseltine' appear on the internal television monitor above my head. "Good Lord! Does that mean that Michael Heseltine is speaking?"

"Yes, he's the Secretary of State, replying for the Government in this debate on an environmental issue," I replied.

"He's such a great speaker. Is there any chance we could listen to him?"

"Not if you want your pudding," I advised discouragingly. "Well, Michael (Welsh Guards and now The Lord Heseltine) is certainly a great speaker and always brings our Party Conference to its feet. He has spoken in my constituency once or twice, and is a great favourite with the female 'Burghers' of Winchester. However, he will not be delivering any oratory tonight."

"What do you mean?"

"He will merely be winding up a minor debate by mouthing some very uninspiring civil servant's verbiage. The Chamber will be almost deserted, everyone's gone home. There will only be Mr. Speaker (George Thomas, the late Lord Tonypandy), Michael, the Opposition spokesman, two or three Members and a dog. It will be very boring."

"I'd love to watch it, if we can."

"Okay, but we should go now. Actually, you might be quite interested to see Black Rod come down from the House of Lords to summon Mr. Speaker and the Sergeant at Arms (Lieutenant Colonel Sir Peter Thorne, KCVO, CBE, ERD, Grenadier Guards) to attend the Lords to surrender the Royal Mace and so close Parliament for the holidays.'

"Sounds great, can we go?"

I managed to get two tickets for the Strangers' Gallery and we were given front-row seats, luckily as it turned out.

"There are a lot of people watching for a boring session, aren't there?" my guest remarked.

"Yes, it is very full, but I do not think the public is aware that these are the closing minutes. They certainly haven't come to attend an epic debate."

"Maybe to listen to Heseltine?"

"Possibly, but I think they will be disappointed, this is no occasion for a great speech."

As the debate droned on, I pointed out the guide-dog of a blind Member sitting on the Opposition benches. "Good Lord, John, you weren't joking when said 'two or three Members and a dog' were you?"

"Oh, no, great choreography, old boy, don't you think?" I bragged, as we stifled our laughter.

The debate was due to end at 10.00 pm sharp. At about 9.55 pm I turned to my guest and whispered "it'll be over in five minutes. Michael is now about to start his final *pirouette*. It could contain some fighting words."

"Oh good, let's hope so."

To my amazement, Michael Heseltine, far from winding into some fighting words, remained very low key as he very slightly changed the subject and placed a Motion before the House. Clearly he hoped that it would go through, unobserved, 'on the nod', without a vote being called.

In seconds I realised that I was not alone in seeing what Michael Heseltine was trying to achieve in the sleepy closing moments of Parliament. The Opposition spokesman immediately sprung to his feet and objected in the strongest terms to what he described as, 'a total abuse of the procedures of the House!' On a Point of Order he asked the Minister to withdraw the Motion, 'that he had surreptitiously slid onto the table!' Michael Heseltine did not see it as a Point of Order, so he refused staunchly. As this shouting match progressed the Chamber filled rapidly with Socialist Members who shouted wildly in vehement support for their spokesman. The Speaker shouted "Order! Order! Order!" but, despite increasing gusto, his efforts were in vain. The shouting match increased, both in volume and intensity.

It soon became clear the Socialists had achieved a Parliamentary 'ambush'. When, after Prime Minister's Questions at 3.30 that afternoon, they had waved 'good-bye' to their Conservative colleagues, they had *not gone* home! They had successfully encouraged the Conservatives to leave London while they stayed 'hidden' in offices and flats. Obviously some Socialist-inclined civil servant in Heseltine's department had tipped-off the Socialist Whips' Office and the ambush was laid.

The Socialist ambush was extremely well executed: they appeared in numbers that totally overwhelmed any errant Conservatives who had stayed in the House. According to a well-laid plan, the Socialists soon had the entire Chamber sealed off, with fierce piquets at every door and large 'bouncers' physically threatening the Minister. As the noise and commotion increased the Speaker asked to be let out and was released, unmolested.

It was now about 10.05 pm and the Lord Chancellor was seated on the Woolsack as 'Speaker' of the House of Lords. At 10.00 pm precisely he had dispatched Black Rod to summon Mr. Speaker and the Sergeant at Arms to bring their Royal Mace from the House of Commons to the Lords for onward passage to Buckingham Palace.

Escorted by two Ushers from the Lords, Black Rod, a retired Admiral, in gold chain of office and smart knickerbockers, approached the main doors of the Commons in the customary slow and stately fashion. As was also customary, the doors were slammed in his face to show the 'independence' of the Commons. Following normal form, Black Rod raised his staff and struck the doors firmly. Normally, a fine looking Commons Usher (sometimes a Grenadier) would open a small barred window and ask, "Who goes there?" Black Rod would reply in a clear and stately voice, "Black Rod, on behalf of Her Majesty, Queen Elizabeth the Second, requests entry to this noble House!" On this occasion, however, the bright red face of a Socialist Member of Parliament appeared through the window. He greeted a shocked Black Rod with the ubiquitous and richly earthy words "F*** Off!" The fierce cry echoed around the silenced halls of Parliament like a rifle shot. Black Rod and his Ushers shivered. Peering down the long passage from the Woolsack the Lord Chancellor looked concerned.

Inside the Chamber of the Commons and, I might add, the Strangers' Gallery, a roar of laughter broke out as the earthy words echoed from the doorway. This was too much for the Solicitor General for Scotland (the late Right Honourable Sir Nicholas Fairburn, QC. MP), a fiery and gutsy Tory Minister. Clearly he had had a very good dinner and had been swept into the Chamber, along with a *tsunami* wave of Socialist Members. Red faced, he rose to his feet from the front bench below the gangway and advanced towards the angry picket-line of Socialist members at the Bar of the House. As he came close, he waved his arm and shouted at them, "Out of my way! Out of my way!" At that moment a large, gnarled fist met him squarely on the jaw. He staggered and fell backwards - onto the main floor of the Chamber and lay spread-eagled, like a crucifix. A raucous roar of applause rang out from the Socialist Members as a couple of Conservatives grabbed our Minister under the armpits, dragged him up onto their bench and, as he mumbled incoherently, slapped his face in an effort to bring him round. From his ringside seat my guest was excited beyond imagination. Smiling gratefully he turned to me and said, "Good God, John, do you call this boring?"

In the minutes that followed, Michael Heseltine agreed to withdraw his Motion. Order was restored. Mr. Speaker returned and the Royal Mace was escorted to an astonished, irritated but much relieved House of Lords. Parliament was closed, just a little late!

Chapter 34

Grenadier, 'Big Mac'--
At A Sultan's Luncheon

Eaton Square, mid 1980s

One of my greatest friends in the House of Commons was The Right Honourable Julian Amery, MP (later The Lord Amery), with whom I went on a number of foreign trips, each of them memorable. A master at seeing everything that mattered, he once famously remarked, "John you must never be caught in bed with either a dead woman or a live boy!" He was a dashing member of SOE in the Second World War and, in many ways, a man of a bygone age. His father, Leo, served as Secretary of State for India and Burma in Winston Churchill's wartime administration. Julian was, I believe, the last English owner of a complete house in Eaton Square and a great gourmet. He gave some fantastic entertainment at his London home with the most interesting of people. Julian was also the son-in-law of former Prime Minister the Right Honourable Harold Macmillan OM (Grenadier Guards, and later The Earl of Stockton, who served in The Regiment in the Great War. This episode of his life is brilliantly recorded in a new book by Simon Ball entitled The Guardsmen*). The 'Big Mac', as we knew him, was always full of good stories and fine observations.*

In the mid 1980's Julian invited me to one such small gourmet luncheon. The guest of honour was the Sultan of Oman, a former Sandhurst graduate. An earlier British government had determined that he should take over from his overly traditional father who kept slaves, for example. To achieve this objective, the government contrived a successful and bloodless coup. The three principal British players in that coup were also present at the dining table: The Right Honourable Harold Macmillan OM (Prime Minister on the day of the Omani coup); The Right Honourable The Lord (Alec, Douglas) Home, KT (then Foreign Secretary and later, Prime Minister) and The Right Honourable Julian Amery MP (then Colonial Secretary). Others present were the Omani Ambassador, myself and Viscount (Robert) Cranborne MP (now The Marquis of Salisbury and elder brother of Major The Lord Valentine Cecil, Grenadier Guards). Robert Cranborne's grandfather, 'Roberty' Cranborne, whose family home, Hatfield House, was the venue for the first secret 'tank' trials, served in the First World War with Harold Macmillan and two other future Conservative Cabinet Ministers, Captain Oliver Lyttelton, DSO and Captain Harry Cruickshank. They were all in the 'elite' 2nd Battalion Grenadier Guards, under the legendary command of Lieutenant-Colonel G.D. 'Ma' Jeffreys. Winston Churchill, ejected from the War Cabinet in disgrace after the fiasco in the Dardanelles, was attached to this battalion in late October 1915 to 'learn the ropes of trench warfare' from the legendary Colonel 'Ma'. 'Roberty' Cranborne later served in Winston Churchill's Second World War cabinet alongside Leo Amery.

In the late 1980s, members of our Conservative Defense Committee were invited to the former Cabinet War Rooms, before they were smartened up and structurally adapted for public viewing. It was quite dramatic, because the chambers were *exactly* as they had been left in 1945, with rubbers, pencils and other writing materials on the War Cabinet table. The usher, who was retiring, had merely covered them with a large plastic map sheet, to preserve them for posterity in their exact positions. Our party numbered only five: Sir Anthony Buck OC, MP (Chairman); Winston Churchill MP (Vice-Chairman); Julian Amery MP; The Viscount (Robert) Cranborne MP (Joint Secretary) and myself (Joint Secretary). Of our five names, three were on the nameplates, still in their original places on the table: Churchill; Amery; and Cranborne! As the French say, "The more it changes, the more it stays the same."

Harold Macmillan was at his best at the luncheon. He spoke in a very Churchillian voice, holding the Sultan mesmerized as he described how he had negotiated the Bermuda Agreement, which gave Great Britain 'joint-key' control of the Titan nuclear missiles, based in the United Kingdom. As you may remember, Robert MacNamara (US Secretary of Defense) was very strongly opposed to any British control of US missiles. In essence, Macmillan described it as follows: "Luckily, Jack (Kennedy) and I got on extremely well on a personal level. That is always important in foreign relations and especially so when the Special Relationship between our two countries is concerned. At breakfast, Jack and I dined together with our top advisors. Everyone attended luncheon, it was a 'bun fight'. But in the evening, we dined alone. It was then that the 'relationship' shone. We would run over the main problems to be faced the next day. Very subtly and by means of clever, sophisticated but indirect hints, Jack would guide me as how best to out-manoeuvre MacNamara the following day. The result was that we achieved an historic agreement that caused the Soviets serious problems, particularly in calculating the precise process of decision-making in preparation for a strategic nuclear missile launch. They had to watch and to calculate the vital will and the political pressures upon not one, but two, democratic leaders. It was far more than twice as complex." It might, I submit, be termed as the 'reaction synergy' of Mass Mutual Destruction. If my memory serves, there might have been two other Grenadiers present at this strategically epic conference the Governor, Major-General Sir Julian Gascoigne (a superb public speaker) and his ADC, Captain John Smiley (later Colonel Sir John, Baronet).

I found myself flatteringly placed next to Macmillan when, subsequently, he turned the conversation to Saudi Arabia. We discussed a certain lack of top management drive by the British in the area. I remember him saying, "Most British executives appear unwilling to undergo the hardships of travel in Saudi Arabia. They content themselves by sending out their Second or even Third eleven members. Then wonder why they lose out to the competition. At Macmillan's, I always travel out to Saudi Arabia myself. The Saudis are flattered and indeed almost thankful that I do so. And that is why most of the books in Saudi schools are published by Macmillan! Must send your top people if you expect to deal with top people and get top results."

This epic luncheon stretched well into the afternoon. I did not want it to end, but at about 3.45 pm, the Sultan rose and left for Wimbledon. Some fifteen minutes later, Harold Macmillan, well into his eighties, rose to return to the office! What a Grenadier!

Chapter 35

A "Singing War' and the Captain's Round

St James's Palace, mid 1980's

Dinner on Queen's Guard is always fun and, sometimes, epic fun. I was invited one night by one of my greatest Grenadier friends (in view of what transpired, no names, no pack drill, save to say that I am most proud to be a godfather to his eldest son). The guest of honour was The Right Honourable Harold Macmillan OM. Another distinguished guest was General Sir David Frazer (Grenadier Guards). The Captain of the Queen's Life Guard decided to attend dinner that night and took his traditional place on the right of the Captain of the Queen's Guard. That meant that, as a Member of Parliament, I had the thrill of sitting, on the left, one down from the Captain and next to 'Big Mac'. By then, I knew him quite well, thanks to his son-in law, Julian Amery. It was always a thrill to sit within earshot of 'Big Mac' because he was a superb raconteur *in the Churchill class, full of the most wonderful stories. I remember two, in particular, from that night.*

The conversation turned to the First World War, of which 'Big Mac' was an illustrious veteran. Indeed, he was hit at various times in the head, hand and then in the face (staying at his post in the trenches, and impressing his Commanding Officer mightily). Finally, near Ginchy, on the Somme, he was hit in the knee, but carried on in that perilous assault, only to be felled moments later by a horrible shell wound in the back. He was in the 2nd, 'elite' Battalion, Grenadier Guards, part of the Guards Division that the

Germans christened the 'Iron Division'. 'Big Mac' had some wonderful observations, some of them most ably recorded in Simon Bell's previously mentioned new book *The Guardsmen.* Amongst these observations, some of which I have sadly forgotten, he made an extraordinary but vividly descriptive comment. Asked by the Captain what he saw as the main differences between the two world wars, he replied, "You know one of the most obvious front-line differences between the two world wars was singing!"

"Singing, Sir, what do you mean?" asked the Captain, to his right hand.

"Well, in the Great War, we marched almost everywhere. There was very little transport, particularly near the forward trenches. And besides, there were few roads left, and for much of the time mud was everywhere. We marched, and while we did so we sang. Even in training, we marched most of the time and the marching songs were well known, to both officers and men. When out of contact with the enemy everyone sang as they marched. In the Second World War all this changed. Everyone had masses of transport. There was relatively little marching when out of contact with the enemy and relatively very little singing."

Later, the conversation turned to politics and the influence of the media. In commenting, 'Big Mac' said, "You know, the power of the modern media is enormous and no longer limited to the Great Nations; it's world wide. In the old days, one would travel to some distant land and people would ask one about the great affairs of state: what was the view of the Prime Minister, the American President and what of the activities of the Monarch? Today, it's all very different. The other day, my grandson visited Tibet and Nepal. After travelling in numerous aeroplanes and buses he arrived, travel weary but exhilarated, at Katmandu, high in the Himalayas. He expected to be asked about affairs of State and was stunned by the first question, 'What has happened to Cecil Parkinson?' Well, it was indeed an affair, but hardly an affair of State!"

It was certainly a memorable dinner, but all was not yet over. Once the senior guests had departed we sat down to savour some of the memorable Grenadier observations of the

Great 'Mac' and of David Frazer. This went on for some time and a certain quantity of port and brandy was consumed, even by the Captain (hence no names, no pack drill!). He suddenly proposed that I should carry out his Round of the sentries. The effect of the port was to engender general support for this outrageous proposal. With some heavy huffing and puffing, I was dressed in the Captain's uniform and must say I was very flattered that I could get into his blue trousers, doing up *all* the buttons! But what else would you expect of one of Margaret's hounds? Once downstairs, I went to inspect the Captain's Patrol in Engine Court. The Company Sergeant Major and the Drummer had been well briefed and carried out their duties without a murmur or a slip. To my surprise, the two Escorts were not Guardsmen, but the Ensign and the Buckingham Palace Guard Commander, both dressed at Guardsmen! Thanks to my having endured endless drills, extra piquets and guards when serving in the Regiment the drill came back to me instantly. Apart from a few sentries who began to wonder if the Captain's face was really the same as the one with whom they had mounted guard, all went with out a hitch. We retired to the mess. The Company Sergeant Major was duly invited and we all had some great laughs. I should add however, for the record of duty, that security at St James's remained totally intact.

Footnote:

Not long afterwards, Harold Macmillan was elevated to the peerage, as The Earl of Stockton. I watched his installation in the House of Lords. The Prime Minister, Margaret Thatcher, sat on the Steps of the Throne, as a Privy Council Member and the House filled. It was memorable to see a great, aged Grenadier veteran honoured so, in the Autumn of his years.

Chapter 36

A Grenadier Minister's Return

New Year's Eve, 1980

In the past I had been invited by Roone Arledge, head of ABC's News and Sport, to give a number of television interviews. To that date, the most exciting had been with an Argentine Minister at the outbreak of the Falklands War. However, like several other stories, it has no Grenadier connections and is therefore not included here. However, Roone had been pleased and I had got to know him.

On New Year's Eve, 1980 I received a surprise telephone call at my father's home in the West Country. It was from Roone Arledge. He was in London.

"John, I have flown over to London on a most urgent and important project and I need your help."

"May I ask for some background?"

"Very briefly, we have reason to believe certain rumours that the Iranian Government may be prepared to release the American Hostages next month. Evidently the British Foreign Office has been instrumental, but neither your Government nor ours will say anything."

"How can I help you?"

"Can you get me an interview with your Foreign Secretary?"

"Roone, I trust you know it's New Year Day tomorrow?"

"Of course I do. I would not be over here myself if it were not vitally important."

"Well, in England everyone leaves for home on New Year's

Eve. That will include all Ministers, even Margaret Thatcher. Whitehall will be empty already, except for emergency staff."

"John, this is vitally important and time sensitive. Trust me."

"Ok, I'll see what I can do, but do not expect anything until after the holiday."

"Thank's, John. I knew you'd try, at least. You can contact me here."

I put the telephone down, collected myself and I rang the Foreign Office to get Lord Carrington's home number. I then telephoned him.

True to his Grenadier Heritage, Lord Carrington was well up to emergency situations, even on New Year's Eve. "All right, so long as you think he is *bona fide,* John, I'll come up tomorrow."

"I do know him quite well. When he says it is confidential, I would trust him. He would not have flown over here if it were not extremely important, but I do not know exactly what he will ask you."

"I understand, John. I think I know what he wants, but I want only you and him to be present. No one else. Is that perfectly clear?"

"Absolutely."

"I'll see you in my office at eleven o'clock tomorrow morning. All right?"

" Your office in the Lords or the Foreign Office?"

"In the Foreign Office, at eleven o'clock."

"Fine. Thank you so much, Peter."

"See you tomorrow, and a Happy New Year!"

"Thank you and a Happy New Year to you also, Goodbye."

I ruminated for a brief moment, thinking how Peter Carrington, for one, had certainly not lost his Grenadier standards and sense of discipline.

I telephoned Roone Arledge, who was elated. He asked if his anchorman, Peter Jennings, could join us.

"I know Peter Jennings is very good and very reliable, but no! Lord Carrington gave very special and definite instructions on this. He's doing you a very great favour. Don't upset him."

"OK, see you tomorrow."

"Yes at the main Whitehall entrance of the Foreign Office at half past ten tomorrow morning, you alone!"

"Ok, great."

Early on New Year's morning, I drove back to London, parked my motor car at the House of Commons, much to the surprise of the police, and walk over to met Roone Arledge at the Foreign Office.

Roone Arledge and I were escorted up the grand staircase of the Foreign Office to one of the grandest offices I have ever seen, that of the Secretary of State for Foreign Affairs. Waiting with his secretary, I was amazed to see none other than Peter Jennings, who I had expressly said could not attend. Rune Arledge also appeared surprised. But the fact that he asked me to plead with Lord Carrington told be that he was up to his neck in the 'plot'. However, there was no sense in becoming petulant, so I asked to see Lord Carrington alone. Once in his splendid office I explained the situation. He asked me if I knew Peter Jennings and a little about him. I explained that I knew him only slightly, but vouched for his character and, on that basis, Lord Carrington agreed that he could attend. They were called in and I introduced them.

It may still risk indiscretion to mention the details of the conversation or even the information that was exchanged. But suffice it to say that Roone Arledge was extremely impressed; indeed I might say that he was actually thrilled. In the event, the American hostages were indeed released a few days later, about 30 minutes *after* the *new* American President, Ronald Reagan, was sworn in.

Life was really quite exciting in those days. The Foreign Office had excelled itself, thanks to the leadership of a very sophisticated Grenadier, with two extremely influential Americans as witnesses. It was all part of oiling the wheels of the Anglo-American Special Relationship, the corner-stone of our national defense strategy for almost a century. It has proved to be the vital foundation stone of the Allied cause in both world wars, of the United Nations, throughout the Cold

War and even today in the global ideological struggle against violent extremism. I believe that history may well record the Special Relationship, which today also involves the sovereign Commonwealth nations of Australia, New Zealand and Canada, as the greatest single influence for 'Peace with Freedom' for the whole of the 20th Century. Quite a tribute, but well deserved in any case.

Territorial Army
1st Infantry Brigade (NCB) exercises in Denmark
1980's
Major John Browne MP, serving as a Bde Liason Officer

Chapter 37

Territorial Army-
"You Have to Vote, Sir!"

School of Infantry, Warminster, 1982

I have always had the very highest respect for The Regiment and for all its members, both past and present. I was inspired by its standards and, like all other Grenadiers, tried hard to apply them. I enjoyed my time as a Grenadier so much that when I became a Member of Parliament and could manage my own time I resolved to try to re-join The Regiment, as a Territorial. It would also be interesting to be both Secretary of the Conservative Defense Committee and at the same time up at the 'sharp end' of the Army. Of course, there was no Territorial element in the Household Brigade and there never had been one. Undaunted, I decided to try in the belief that 'nothing ventured, nothing gained'.

ogether with John Magnay (Grenadier Guards, and my former Adjutant), I was invited to be a Financial Advisor to the Household Brigade Funds. The charming Major-General Desmond Langley (Life Guards) was The Major General commanding London District. I explained my plan to him at one of our Trustees' meetings in his office at Horse Guards. He was very interested and asked me to keep in touch with my progress. I duly wrote a formal letter. To my dismay, I received a letter from the Brigade Major, London District (a young Major Erskin-Crum, the son of my Commandant when I was a recruit at Caterham). He told me that the Guards do not have Territorials and suggested that I tried to join the Greenjackets, in my Winchester constituency!

Over coffee, before we sat down to our next Trustees' meeting, I told Desmond Langly of my disappointing status. "Leave it to me, John. I'll be in touch with you."

A few minutes later, as we sat around a large conference table, there was a loud explosion in the distance. If I remember correctly, it even appeared to shake the windows at Horse Guards. The Major General left the room to determine what had happened. Moments later he returned with a terrible look on his face. The explosion was caused by a nail-bomb, placed by the IRA that caused carnage to the Life Guard, then passing the back of the old Hyde Park hotel, on their way to mounting Guard at Horse Guards. The Life Guard Commander was Desmond Langley's godson. He was killed. One of the surviving chargers was dear 'Sefton' who was outrageously maimed, but became an animal superstar during his recovery. Naturally, our meeting was adjourned, immediately.

A week or two later, I received a telephone call from The Major General. "John, I have been authorized by highest authority to tell you that you may be badged as a Grenadier, Volunteer. That means that you must wear a letter 'V' below your badges of rank!" It was the greatest of news. How wheels work! I immediately applied to join the Territorial Army. After a medical and an interview, I was accepted and pulled out my old uniforms. They were however, somewhat tight! Actually, it worked well, because, there were other Guardsmen who wanted to join the Territorial Army, but were not prepared to join another regiment. My old friend Philip Wright, now a Deputy Sergeant at Arms in the House of Commons, followed suit as a Grenadier Volunteer.

I was posted, as a watch keeper to 1st Infantry Brigade at Tidworth, on the western border of my constituency. It was a fully independent, immediate response brigade of some 17,000 men. I thought it could not be better, but I was wrong. Firstly, the Brigade was soon to be commanded by one of my greatest friends and Best Man, Brigadier Willie Rous OBE (later, as Lieutenant-General the Honourable Sir William Rous KCB, OBE, he became Colonel of the Coldstream Guards). We had both been in Marne Company at Sandhurst, had stayed often in each other's homes and had been on many School of Infantry courses together. I had also taken over the Signal responsibilities from him in British Guiana in June 1963. If that were not thrill enough, I then gained a place on the Battle Group Commander's Course at the School of Infantry at Warminster. All was going swimmingly when, amazingly, Argentina invaded the Falkland Islands. I was asked to do a live debate with an Argentine Minister that Friday night on ABC's Nightline program. There followed on Saturday morning one of the most exciting debates ever in the House of Commons. Unbelievably, the chance of active service loomed. I immediately volunteered, as I did for Rhodesia and for the First Gulf War. However, the Government clearly did not want the eyes of any prying MP near the 'front'. In each case, the Tory Minister said that no elements of the TA would be deployed. Of course, this proved to be untrue, both in the Falklands and in the Gulf. Sadly, it was not the only lie they told. Nevertheless, life in Parliament was not without its excitement at that time. For example, in between debates, I was, on one occasion shipped, as the only official passenger, by Concorde to do a Rodger Mudd special television interview for NBC in Washington.

I was posted to Warminster on my Battle Group Commander's course. All the while juggling time with the House, so as not to fail to be present for the all-important 'war votes.' The course provided great revision of all I had forgotten since leaving The Regiment and also a lot of new wisdom.

One important event on the Warminster course was the major 'Defense' exercise. I was in charge of a platoon on this exercise and we were 'dug in' on Salisbury Plain. All was quite tense as we peered out of our trenches, expecting an attack at, or before, last light. There was an eerie silence and we were all keyed-up, Suddenly, I heard a 'stage whispered' voice from one of the Directing Staff. I thought I heard my name. What was wrong, I thought? "Major Browne. Major Browne. Are you here, Sir?"
"Yes, I'm over here, Staff, " I replied, also in a stage whisper.
"You have to come with me, Sir."

"Why?"

"There is going to be a vote in Parliament tonight."

"What?"

"Yes, you have to vote, Sir. The Government Whips have just telephoned. You have to leave right now, Sir. I have a Land Rover near battle group headquarters."

Well, there was nothing for it. I had to climb out of my trench, hand over to the Platoon Sergeant, give my Sterling sub-machine gun to the Directing Staff and follow him to the field headquarters. He drove me back to Warminster, which took forever, over deep tank-tracks. Once back at the school, I took off my web equipment and jumped into my own motor car.

After a very fast drive to London - before the age of the dreaded speed camera - I made it to the House of Commons, just in time to visit a bathroom and wash the camouflage cream from my face, as the   Division Bell sounded. I had no time to change, so had to vote in combat kit. In doing this, I remembered to take off my badges of rank. This was lucky, as I was extremely tired, but it avoided a scene with any Socialists who would have been sure to raise embarrassing Points of Order had I been spotted in the Commons, wearing anything that might be termed 'Royal Patronage' like badges of rank, with a Major's crown!

After the vote, it was a cup of coffee and back to Warminster to get the duty driver to take me back to my old Platoon position. I was relieved to find that the enemy attack had been successfully repulsed, with no home-side casualties. It was perhaps a good thing after all that, as a chocolate -coated, soft centred MP, I had been well away from the serious action when the balloon had gone up!

Chapter 38

Operation 'Top Hat'

Her army and her navy
Britain shall cast aside;
Soldiers and ships are costly things
Defence an empty pride
—The Fox's Prophecy

House of Commons, 1990

Napoleon is reputed to have said that 'God is on the side of the big battalions'. Of course, he was speaking tactically. History shows that, in terms of total strategy, it is 'will', not size, that is the crucial element. For it is the political 'will' that dictates both the size and, more importantly, the quality of a nation's armed forces.

History also shows that, for many people, 'Peace at any Cost' is indeed the noblest of ideals. However, 'Peace at any Cost' has never been the cry of the British people. For us, the only acceptable peace has been, 'Peace with Freedom'.

With the success of Mr. Gorbachev's meetings with Margaret Thatcher (the 'Iron Lady') the way was opened for him to meet President Reagan. These historic meetings heralded the end of the 'Cold' phase of the Second World War. That, in turn, led certain people to believe that the very nature of the strategic peace, of nuclear deterrence, under which we had all lived for almost half a century, had changed to a peace of nuclear detente. Some even felt that we could therefore swap the threat of mass mutual destruction for the hope of mass mutual trust. This gave some senior politicians the feeling that they could buy some more votes with a massive Peace Dividend. 'Options for Change' (offering no options whatsoever, in reality) was duly introduced by a Conservative Government. Indeed, the atmosphere of euphoria was such that even the Conservative dominated Defense Select Committee felt that the Regimental System could be destroyed with abandon. Clearly they paid little heed to Rudyard Kipling's classic remark that, 'A man may join for King or Country, he goes over the top for the honour of his own platoon, company or battalion'. However, some of us backbenchers felt that the vital precepts of the first two paragraphs in this chapter were being ignored. We felt that a Conservative Opposition would never have allowed Socialist governments to get away with such cuts. Furthermore, the cuts themselves were most un-business-like and socialist in nature. What business would cut evenly across the board, without assessing what avenues of business it wanted to boost and what areas it wished to cut out all together? Furthermore, what business would cut the most profitable areas (bands and the Household Division) by almost double the rate of the general cut? We successfully opposed the destruction of the regimental system, but failed to halt Options for Change. In the meantime, Margaret Thatcher was brought down, like Caesar, by her closest lieutenants in a political sea of blood, knee deep.

One morning, in the months following, the Regimental Adjutant telephoned me with a call from the Lieutenant Colonel, Major-General Bernard Gordon-Lennox. It concerned the woefully inadequate compensation to be paid to three Grenadiers who had been severely wounded. The Lieutenant Colonel accepted my invitation to discuss the details over luncheon in the House that afternoon.

Apparently, the three Guardsmen - Povey, Ray and Hicks - were on a live firing exercise in Canada. They were instructed to dig a mortar pit. Whilst digging, one of their pickaxes struck an unexploded anti-tank shell buried in the ground. It exploded, causing catastrophic injury to the three Grenadiers, all of whom lost their legs. From memory, they were each offered some twenty-three thousand pounds in compensation. I shared General Bernard's view that it was both inhumane and derisory. I told him that I had put my name down to speak that evening in the debate upon the Defense Estimates, including 'Options for Change'. If called upon to speak, I undertook to raise this subject, with gusto.

That afternoon Margaret Thatcher, by then a backbencher, joined three of us for tea at a table in the Members' Tea Room. Naturally, most of the conversation centred around the current defense debate on 'Options for Change'. Needless to say, Mrs. Thatcher agreed with us. As we got up to leave, I said, "Margaret (it was still odd not to address her as Prime Minister), I sincerely hope you are going to vote 'No' tonight?"

"John, how can I?" she exclaimed with great concern. "As I said, I agree with you, but if I, as a former Prime Minister, voted against the Government on their Defense Estimates, there would be uproar! I just can't. I'm not in a position to do so." With that, we all parted. I returned to the Chamber to 'sit-out' my chance of being called. (It is perhaps worth noting that when she did speak out against the Conservatives' policy to sign the Maastricht, European Union, Treaty, John Major retaliated by asking HM The Queen, to make her a Baroness rather than the traditional award of Countess. The Tory Whips can hurt even former Prime Ministers!).

After a further five hours or so of 'knees-bend' exercises, rising repeatedly to be recognized, I was called to speak. I tempered my original speech by cutting out my intended mention that 'Socialism appears to have broken out in the Ministry of Defense', because I was asking a favour of the Government and did not want to ruffle too many feathers. Hansard contains the exact words, but from memory (my *general* words are merely in single, rather than double quotation marks), I asked the Minister (The Honourable Archibald Hamilton, formerly Coldstream Guards and now The Lord Hamilton), 'to give the unfortunate Grenadiers a reasonable, once-off and exceptional settlement'. Sensing his lack of positive response and evasiveness I told him, during an intervention in his summing up speech that 'should the Government delay in acting in a humane manner, I propose to wear my black top hat on every occasion that I sit in this

Chamber, until justice is done.' This threat was laughed out with jeers, led by the duty Whip, at the Minister's side.

The Debate ended with a vote that the Government won with the application of a strict 'Three-Line' whip. However, I voted in the 'No' lobby. As a loyal Tory I hated voting against my Party, but I felt very strongly on this issue. To me it was a point of principle. I was somewhat sad as I was counted out of the 'No' lobby with a bunch of Socialists. However, I was greatly impressed to see Margaret Thatcher waiting outside the lobby doors. Clearly she had crossed the entire length of the House from the 'Aye' lobby exit. She came up to me and with great sadness in her eyes said, "John, you were quite right. We will never, ever, be able to act again in an independent manner, as we did in the Falklands!" I felt enlivened.

When I returned to the House the next day, I took my top hat. A senior Tory Whip accosted me. He was not amused and said, "You're not really going to wear that ridiculous thing in here, are you?"

"I'm going to do as promised, until justice is done."

"Well, it might interest you to know that you are the only Conservative Member to have voted against Conservative Defence Estimates in this entire century. It's tantamount to treason!"

"Treason? Some would call it patriotism. The real traitors are those who are irresponsibly denuding our armed forces, from within!"

"John, you're already in so much trouble, I just don't understand why you bother over this. You're going to wish you'd never been born!"

Well, like true Tory Whips, they subsequently shot to kill and brought my political career to an abrupt, most unceremonious and un-Grenadier like halt following, in my opinion, a political show trial that was worthy of a dictatorship. It was not justice, but it was politics. The tabloids had a field day castigating me as a cad and a cheat. I soon learnt that they would not allow any statement of the true facts to get in the way of a good story, so I have remained silent for almost 20 years. However, to the extent that some Grenadiers may have believed the press reports, I feel that I owe them at least some brief explanation (*see Afterword*). Rest assured, had I felt at any time that I had behaved badly or dishonestly, I would have resigned from my clubs and Regimental associations rather than bring disgrace upon them.

I had always accepted that politics are played with a hard ball. When you try to hit a six and miss the ball, and get hit in the face, it hurts. That is why I worked hard in my Constituency, undertaking over 300 events each year. In the old days, I would have ended up on the scaffold or with my wine being officially poisoned. However, in those more modern times, the poison was merely handed out by the Government Whips for the media to deliver. I ended up living in exile but, thanks to the Grenadiers, I survived. Some 16 years later I still feel I did my duty of placing Country before Party and would do exactly the same again.

The first arrow in the quiver of the Tory Whips is ridicule. True to form, the first time I wore my top hat in the chamber some Government Whips' backbench lackeys were instructed to carry out the ridicule. I remember one 'Butter Mountain' MP shouting out, "John, take that ridiculous hat off. You look so bloody stupid wearing it." He was greeted with roars of Tory supportive laughter. Not much fun when you are an enthusiastic Tory.

A day or two later, I was approached by some of those wonderful House Door Keepers, mostly senior Warrant Officers from the armed forces. In this case, they included a Coldstreamer, a 60th Rifleman and a Royal Marine. They were led by a former Corporal of Horse in the Life Guards (to avoid any threat to their pension status, no names, no pack drill). The Corporal of Horse took me aside and said, "Sir, we have it on good authority that your Whips are on a 'seek and destroy' mission. They want to get your hat! They're looking for it everywhere. They're so mad they'll destroy it when they find it and I understand black top hats are hard to come by these days. But never fear, Sir. The Guards won't let you down."
"What do you mean?"
"Well, Sir. Do you see this panel here, Sir?" He pushed a

small panel aside in the oak panelling behind the Speaker's Chair to reveal emergency medical and oxygen equipment. "We're going to hide it in here for you, Sir. You just hand it to us, quiet like and we'll handle the rest. When you come in and want it, just give us the 'wink'. Sound alright, Sir?"

"Sounds great to me. Like the blind side of a rugby scrum, what?"

"Spot on, Sir."

During the next few days media interest heightened and the Government was increasingly angry as I stepped up my lobbying. The Tory whips were becoming extremely frustrated. I always had my top hat in the chamber but once outside it was nowhere to be seen, on no head or coat-peg, anywhere in the entire palace of Westminster.

The only real apparent downside was that Mr. Speaker would not call me to speak, even in Business Questions, when it was his custom to call every one who stood. It was a clear abuse of power and most tiresome. After some three weeks I rose on a Point of Order, on Business Questions. Again, Hansard will have the exact words, but I remember words to the effect, 'Mr. Speaker, with all due respect, I have been standing continuously now for some three weeks and have failed to catch your eye? Was it because I was wearing my top hat?'

'Well, it is true that I do find it rather hard to recognise the Honourable Gentleman under the shadow of the hat!' (roars of laughter). Once the next debate was under way Mr. Speaker (subsequently,The Right Honourable The Lord Weatherill) beckoned me to The Chair. "John, it is true that I have not called you because of your hat and that is very wrong. In fact your Whips asked me to order you to take it off. But I told them that it has been a legitimate form of dress in here for over 150 years and, anyway, how can I possibly order you to take it off when I'm sitting here in a tri-corn hat and a wig?"

"Quite so, Mr. Speaker."

"John, I'll tell you what I'll do. I'll call you if you undertake not to wear your hat while you're actually speaking."

"Of course Mr. Speaker, I know the rules."

"Good. You'll be called," he added, with a knowing smile and a wink.

A few days later I rose to ask a question and was duly called. Taking off my hat I put my question. A neighbouring backbench Member, with an eye for fun, could not contain himself. He moved my hat. I sat down firmly... right, smack bang on my top hat and to roars of laughter from the House and from the Press and Public galleries! This was all too much for the television. I might have been a new king alighting a throne for the first time. My 'sitting' was played over and over again for hours, even days. It all added great publicity. However, my poor top hat was by then most certainly only good for weddings!

As the publicity mounted, my lobbying was increasingly well received in certain political quarters. Apparently, it rose to fever pitch when Americans watching Prime Minister's Questions on C Span TV, asked the local British High Commissions in various States, 'Why is that man, sitting behind the Prime Minister, wearing a black top hat?' Evidently the waves of inquiry were all routed via the British Embassy in Washington to the Foreign Office in London. It was all getting rather embarrassing. Then, apparently, a Canadian opposition MP, clearly seeking to embarrass his government, asked, 'Why, if this accident occurred on Canadian soil, is the Canadian government not giving the British Grenadiers fair compensation?' What would be next? Would the Queen be called upon for a ruling between two Commonwealth Members? It was the final straw and it broke the Whitehall camel's back. Within days the Grenadiers were given a once-off award of seven hundred and fifty thousand pounds.

Subsequently, Guardsman Povey, doing marvellously well on his new legs and looking every inch a Grenadier warrior, joined me to inspect the British Legion, Hampshire Colours Parade, in my Constituency.

Footnote:
That top hat must have earned more money than any that Mr. Lock ever made! Who said that being old-fashioned "don't work" these days?

Part Nine

AUTUMN YEARS

As they say, growing old
is not for the faint hearted!

Chapter 39

"Foreign Berries, Sir!"

Boodles Club, London, Summer 1996

Boodles Club has no formal ties to the Grenadier Guards, although it does have many Grenadier members and its Roll of Honour depicts the names of many Guardsmen, including a high number of Grenadiers, killed in the service of our Country in both World Wars. By tradition, the Queen's Company Dinner is held at Boodles. I was also pleased, the other day, to see two Grenadier officers taking tea at Boodles, dressed in Guard Order. Despite the fact that there are no official ties, there are strong Grenadier associations. I therefore feel able to include a Boodle's story in this book.

In the Summer of 1996 Boodles celebrated the 100th anniversary of its financial independence from the descendants of the original club proprietor, Edwin Boodle. A grand Ball was held at Sion House, the London home of the Duke of Northumberland. It was superbly organized for some one thousand guests. My old Sandhurst compatriot, Field Marshal The Lord Guthrie (Welsh Guards and SAS) took the salute at Tattoo, which was sounded by Guards bands. It was all superbly administered, with Boodle's staff on hand at every corner to assist with any problem.

The following day, we were decanted to our wonderful 'sister' club, White's, in order to give Boodle's time to reorganize. At White's I enjoyed some English summer pudding. The next day we were back at Boodle's. However, I noticed that there was no summer pudding on the menu. So, I spoke to the manager of the coffee room saying, "Luciano, I see there's no English summer pudding on the menu today."

"Indeed no, Sir," he replied.

"But I had English summer pudding at White's yesterday. How can we be beaten to the post by White's?"

"Foreign berries, Sir!"

"Foreign berries?"

"Yes Sir. Apparently, the chef at White's is prepared to use imported fruit!"

Chapter 40

A Grenadier Path to 'The Tiger'

The Open Championship, St Andrews, 2000

There is a personality and a style about the great sportsmen which marks them out irrespective of generation. Thus Tiger Woods is one of the acknowledged 'greats' of golf. The best judges who have seen him rank him in the company of the immortal Bobby Jones and Jack Nicklaus. In addition, he is now expected to be the first athlete in history to make a billion dollars in sport from his own hand and related endorsements. Still a young man, he is already a legend. He is, truly, a living legend. For a 'golf nut' like me to exchange even a few words with Tiger Woods would be like a 'Bobby Soxer' speaking to the 'King'- the one and only Elvis Presley. I did not scream but, as one who has all too often felt the full and savage humiliation of golf, I did experience the great thrill of speaking to probably the greatest golfer that has ever lived.

I had the strong feeling in 2000 that Tiger Woods would complete his personal Grand Slam at The Open Championship on the hallowed turf of St. Andrews, Scotland.

I was staying near Perth with my old Sandhurst classmate, Lieutenant Colonel Stephen Lindsay (The Black Watch) and his wonderful wife, Annie. It was already a memorable week because their youngest son, Andrew, had just been selected for the Gold Medal-winning British Olympic Eights Boat, to race in Australia.

I travelled from Perth to Leuchers by train. Opposite me sat a golf enthusiast who had a number of golf articles spread out before him on the table that separated us. They contained many dramatic golf diagrams. Sensing my curiosity he kindly explained to me that they depicted the scoring of the first 'Albatross' in professional golf in America. An Albatross is a score of three under par in a single hole. In this case the player had hit a ball over 400 yards (normally done, at par, in four shots) and into the hole in just one shot! It was spectacular and provided much discussion. We made friends. As we were getting off the train he asked me, "Have you ever been to a major golf tournament before?"

"No, I've only watched them on television," I replied.

"Well, you will be the only person in a coat and tie. I suggest you take it off."

I was in a Grenadier boating jacket. It was a hot day and I did not want to walk around carrying a coat, so I kept it on. Of the 52,000 people at St. Andrews, some 10,000 buzzed around Tiger Woods like a swarm of bees. Everywhere that Tiger went the stands were full, including the practice range and putting green. It was very hard, demanding great patience, to get anywhere near him.

As luck would have it, however, the only people amongst the record crowd who wore a coat and tie were the Officers of The Royal and Ancient Golf Club. As I approached stand after stand, anywhere near Tiger Woods, the notices read 'full'. However on many occasions a steward would raise the tape and wave me on shouting, "This way, Sir. Step this way, Sir!" By the time I was level with the steward and he could see that my tie was not that of the Royal and Ancient it was too late and embarrassing for him to turn me back. I got into almost every stand and place I tried, including the practice range. The thrilling result was that I managed a couple of stilted sentences with the great Tiger before he entered the practice putting green.

"Good luck, Tiger!"

"Thanks" he replied.

"Do you think St.Andrews will be lucky for you today?"

"I sure hope so. Saint Andrews is golf history," he said smiling. Then he was off.

On the way back from the putting green he was so focused, it was as if he was in a trance. I have never seen such concentration. It was so powerful that no one even tried to speak to him directly. He went on to win the Open and his personal Grand Slam, holding all four major titles at once, although not in the same calendar year. I managed to see quite a bit of him on the way round. I also witnessed the sad sight of David Duval taking four shots to get out of a wretched bunker at the 17th green. It dropped him from a close second to way down the leaders. On the 18th fairway we were allowed to follow the players from behind a rope. I saw two boys, caught slipping under it, dumped in the bern! Then a female streaker, apparently (I could not see, but would anyway have been too bashful to look!) wearing only a butterfly tattooed onto her right buttock, crossed the 18th green. I understand that she caused a sensation and many ribald comments as male policemen chased after her. Once caught, she received a massive ovation.

In receiving his prize, Tiger Woods thanked every one and said how wonderful it was to have won at St.,Andrews, the home of golf and that his personal grand slam should have culminated at *The* Open!"

Captain Barry Double, conducting the
Grenadier American Battlefield Tour. 2001

Mrs. Angela Winthrop as Myopia with 'Nanny' Chisolm

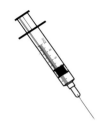

Chapter 41

"De British Bloods No Good!"

West Palm Beach, Florida, September 2004

O n 30th July 2004, Frederic and Susan Winthrop took me to the wedding of a mutual, Kirkwood friend (Amy Kirkwood and Lane Smith) at Shawnee, on the historic banks of the Delaware River. Freddy (formerly US Marine Corps, Agricultural Secretary for Massachusetts and Chairman or the Trustees of the Reservation (forerunners to the English National Trust) was the younger brother of my great friend, the late Adam Winthrop (also former US Marine Corps and a Harvard ice hockey and polo player), with whom I spent many happy months playing polo both in America and in England. As a very good 4-goal handicapped player Adam was the strong man on the medium-goal team that I ran at Windsor in the early 1970's. With his father's approval I named my team Groton House in Adam's honour. I am very proud to be a godfather to Adam's eldest daughter, Angela.

Freddy's mother, Mrs. Angela Winthrop, had several British refugees to live at Groton House for the duration of the Second World War. Assisted by Susie and Freddy she gave a wonderful luncheon party for the entire Grenadier Guards American Battlefield Tour Party, including wives, in September 2001. (The tour was very ably run by Captain Barry Double and Major Bob Woodfield.)

The Grenadiers and their wives were entranced as Freddy, standing below a portrait of General Frederic Winthrop, his kinsman, described how he, aged only 25, had been the last

Union General to be killed in the Virginia campaign of the Civil War. He had fought in every major battle of that campaign, including Gettysburg, when he had absented himself from hospital in order to be with his men. His Corps Commander subsequently paid him the greatest of tributes when he apparently said, "The victory at Five Forks (the last major battle of that campaign) was not worth the death of Frederic Winthrop." Freddy showed the Grenadiers the General's pistol, sword, red sash and even the bullet that killed his forebear. (In those days it was the custom, when possible, to return the bullet to the next of kin). Freddy then showed the Grenadiers two Springfield rifles (one of 1899 origin, the other from 1903) that his own father, the late Frederic Winthrop (formerly a Lieutenant Colonel in the US Army, serving in the Pacific), had sent to England at the outbreak of the Second World War. Both rifles were subsequently returned, each with an inscribed plaque on the butt which read 'This rifle was loaned to us for the defense of Britain in a time of dire necessity. It is now returned to its owner Frederic Winthrop with our grateful thanks.' It makes one realize the true depth of the 'Special Relationship' between the United Kingdom and the United States, one that has given us both the great freedom and much of the enterprise that we all now enjoy.

I was staying with Angela Winthrop in August 2005, starting to write this book, when she gave me an old copy of *The Times* newsheet which she had found in her extensive files, which include memories of her visits aboard HMS *Hood*, the pride of the Royal Navy. Subsequently, the *Hood* was tragically and dramatically sunk by the *Bismarck* in the North Atlantic, with only a handful of survivors out of over one thousand souls. An interesting parallel was that at Malvern we had an outstanding Royal Marine instructor, QMSI D.W. Gasson, BEM. 'Gas' was a lynch-pin in our CCF. When serving aboard *HMS Invincible*, at the Battle of Jutland in 1916, he was blown up with his gun-turret as the ship exploded. Remarkably, he was one of only five survivors – the remaining crew of over a thousand were all lost.

Mrs. Winthrop's copy of *The Times* was historic, embossed in red on the top right hand corner were the words, 'END OF

WAR IN EUROPE'. It was dated 8th May 1945, the day following the defeat of Germany in the Second World War. It contained some remarkable items, some of them Grenadier-related. On the amusing side it was amazing, on such a dramatic and historic day, to read the headline of the stock market segment. It read, 'Generally Dull'. Also on such a historic day it was interesting to note an announcement in the Court Circular that 'Anne, Lady Cory has returned to 28 Belgrave Square from the country'. Reading these two statements lent a certain authenticity to the remark reported by a shaken American news correspondent on The Western Front in 1916. Evidently, he encountered a platoon of Coldstreamers being drilled on the parapet of a reserve trench under the gaze of a young officer. Apparently he approached the young officer saying, "Don't you realize that there's a war on?"

The young Coldstreamer is alleged to have replied, "In the history of the Coldstream Guards, war is merely another incident!"

On the Grenadier front, there was both good and extremely bad news. The good news was the lead in the Court Circular. It read: 'The Princess Elizabeth today inspected, at Wellington Barracks, the 5th Battalion, Grenadier Guards, the Regiment of which she is Colonel.' A subsequent article reported that the Battalion was commanded by Lieutenant-Colonel E. J. B. Nelson, (Lieutenant-Colonel Huntington having recently been killed in action). The Colonel received Major Philip Sidney, Victoria Cross; four wounded officers, including Captain Gore-Browne (former Adjutant); Lieutenants Wedderburn, Curry and Lynn; and then 10 auxiliary ATS women, working at Regimental Headquarters.[It has long been known that Headquarters get all the luck!]

The bad Grenadier news was tragic in the extreme: on the front page, the parents of a young officer, Terrence Reeves, on the first day of peace, had placed an advertisement saying that their young Grenadier son had been missing in action since April 1945, and asking for any information concerning his whereabouts to be sent to them. Tragically, some few pages later, there lay an announcement that, in addition to the official casualty lists, *The Times* had received notice of the deaths of other officers. The short list included Lieutenant T. Reeves, Grenadier Guards. It was enough to bring tears to the toughest of eyes.

Now, back to my story. At the Kirkwood wedding I was teamed to play golf in a competition with Susie Winthrop's sister Gillian. Sadly, I had picked up some bug. I felt so weak that even lifting a golf club was an effort. I shot a horrendous and unprintable score. I felt very bad because Gillian is a great golfer and I let her down badly. That evening I mentioned it to someone who put me onto an "outstanding doctor" near Palm Beach. I duly made an appointment and was given the most sophisticated of blood tests and examinations.

Upon reviewing the results of my blood test my new doctor asked if I lived near a golf course. I replied with a certain satisfaction, " Yes, I live right next to my golf club!"

To my great surprise she replied, "Well that's the answer to your first problem."

"What do you mean?"

"You have three problems. One is a high concentration of pesticide. It is most probably caused by the pesticide that, through your subscription, you pay for to be applied to your golf course. The second is a high concentration of mercury, most probably due to your amalgam tooth fillings. The third is a high level of iron."

Indignantly, I replied, "Well, I blame the pesticide on golf, the amalgam on the army who put in my fillings and the iron on the Grenadier Guards!"

"What do you mean, the Grenadier Guards?"

Laughingly I replied, "Well the Grenadiers, especially the Guards Depot, make iron men by pumping them full of Grenadier Spirit and iron discipline!"

The doctor laughed and added, "I can recommend a diet and give you some pills for the pesticide and mercury. But you must get rid of three pints of blood, at a blood bank, to reduce you iron levels."

A week or two later I paraded at the West Palm Beach blood bank. I filled in piles of paper and was duly hitched up and laid to rest on a very comfortable bed, with an individual television. I switched into the Golf Channel, as did the man next to me. After some time he rather irritatingly interrupted me to talk. As I replied to his stream of questions a passing nurse wheeled in on me, like a Guards Depot drill instructor who had heard the telltale sound of a dropped rifle. She shouted, "Where are you from?"

"What do you mean?" I asked indignantly.

"You sound like you're British. Are you British?"

"Well, I am English, yes." I replied somewhat pompously. Thank God, she did not ask if I was a European!

"De British bloods no good!" she exclaimed as she somewhat wildly wrenched the needle out of my arm, throwing it and my plastic bag of almost a pint of blood into a disposal bin.

Utterly amazed, I protested, 'It may not be blue, but it is good, old, red, English blood.'

"It's no good!"

" You mean that Jack's giant will no longer cry out, 'fee, fie, foe, fum, I smell the blood of an Englishmun'?" Other donors laughed heartedly, but she looked at me blankly as I was escorted out, somewhat unceremoniously.

The next day I received a telephone call in my office from a charming woman, who introduced herself as the Manager of the blood bank. She apologized profusely for what had happened. "Mr. Browne, you did fill in your forms quite correctly, showing that you were in Great Britain at the time of mad cow disease. My assistant should have noticed it and have been far more apologetic. I have spoken to her since. She won't make the same mistake again. I really am most terribly sorry for what happened to you."

I was quite amazed that anyone would take the trouble to call and apologize, especially in such a charming and honest manner. 'Must be a volunteer' I thought, but then I remembered that this is Palm Beach, after all!

I asked how I was going to get rid of my remaining two pints. Initially she was unable to help but then accepted my suggestion that I build up a blood bank for my own individual use, or for any fellow Englishman who wants to placate Jack's giant! So now, at long last, I am back to a high standard of Grenadier fitness—for my great age that is!

Chapter 42

"That's Not A Salute!"

The footsteps of the invader
Then England's shore shall know,
While home-bred traitors give the hand
To England's every foe

Disarmed before the foreigner,
The knee shall humbly bend,
And yield the treasures that she lacked
The wisdom to defend
                        —The Fox's Prophecy

Barnstaple, Devon, May 2005

In the Spring of 2005, as a Vice-President of the United Kingdom Independence Party (UKIP – in my view, the only Patriotic political party we have left), I stood as their candidate in the General Election for the constituency of North Devon. By coincidence, it was the constituency once held by the Honourable James Lindsay MP, the father of one of my greatest friends and Sandhurst classmates, Lieutenant Colonel Stephen Lindsay (The Black Watch). I had spent many wonderful weekends at his home, Heddon Hall, and, therefore, knew something of the area.

One evening, in early May 2005, I was canvassing a village called Fremington, just outside Barnstaple. As a minor party we did not have the resources to compile proper canvassing cards. In order to cover the ground, we had to canvas 'blind,' without knowing either the identity or the political leaning of the people we canvassed. I knocked on one door and had a very pleasant conversation with the owner. As I left, I gave him a somewhat casual 'semper five' American style salute. "That's not a salute!" he said in obvious disgust. "This, is a *proper* salute" he said firmly, as he whipped his right hand up above his right eye, where it remained, palm forward, for a few seconds, quivering with efficiency, until it was brought smartly down to his side.

"Well, that looks like a Guard's salute to me," I said, smiling in an effort to lessen his disgust.

"It *is* a Guard's salute," he snapped.

"Were you a Guardsmen then?" I enquired.

"Yes, I most certainly was, Irish Guards!" At that moment, the penny dropped.

"Not Sergeant Pittaway?" I enquired eagerly.

"Yes, Edward Pittaway."

"Well, good God, I'm John Browne. You were my squad instructor when I was a junior cadet at Sandhurst."

"B'Jesus, I didn't recongise you, Sir." Shaking hands, he added, " Come inside, Sir. Meet my wife Francis and have a drink." We had a very nostalgic conversation and looked through a lot of his old photographs. Subsequently he gave me a photograph of myself as the Senior Under Officer of Marne Company on the Sandhurst drill competition parade with Major Gilbert Lamb (Grenadier Guards) as the Inspecting Officer. I shall always treasure it. Following the theft of my motor car on leaving Sandhurst it is one of very few photographs I now have of some wonderful days at the Academy.

 # Chapter 43

"Are You in that Mob Then, Guv?"

Taught wisdom by disaster,
England shall learn to know
That trade is not the only gain
Heaven gives to man below
                    —The Fox's Prophecy

London, January 2006

I had an appointment at Wellington Barracks. As my programme was hectic, I took a taxicab. We turned towards Buckingham Palace. As we were circling 'The Birthday Cake' we were stopped by the police to allow the 'New' Queen's Guard to march past. I believe Nijmegen Company were mounting guard that day and that the Captain was Major Marcus Elliott-Square, and the Ensign Lieutenant Benjamin Jesty.

As the Guard marched by, the cab driver turned his head and remarked, "You know, 't's bloody amazin' how they still turn out in such numbers to watch that lot, ain'it, Guv?"
"Well, they're the best on the world aren't they?" I responded.
"If you say so, Guv," replied the cabbie in good-humoured despair.
A few moments later the flow of traffic was restored and we arrived at the Petty France entrance to Wellington barracks. I got out and went to the front window to pay my fare.
"Are you in that mob then, Guv?"
"I *was,*" I replied, smiling.

"Well, take this one on me, Guv. You're right, they *are* a great lot," he replied with a broad smile. With that he drove off.

I was dumbfounded, so much so that I failed to note the taxicab's number. I remembered that, when I was a recruit at Caterham, local bus conductors would often refuse our fares out of sympathy. They were, of course, giving away very small amounts of company money. Why would this cabbie give away six pounds of his own hard-earned money? I believe it was because the Guards are truly loved and respected by the British people. It also shows that a former King and First World War veteran, the late Duke of Windsor, was not alone in his opinion of The Regiment as, "The Best of the Best...Yes...the Best!"

Epilogue

WHAT MAKES A GUARDSMAN?

Tenacitas Victrix

This question must surely have intrigued the minds of many for decades, even centuries. It probably entered the thoughts of German warriors, of the First World War, for they were minded, from the hundreds of allied divisions they faced, to christen the Guards Division, the 'Iron Division'. More recently, it may have prompted many valiant German officers, when surrendering to the Allies at the close of the Second World War, to insist initially that they would surrender their men only to elements of the British Guards. What was it that led to such conclusions? I venture to suggest that it was 'respect'; but respect for what? Looking back at the history of the Guards, whether humorous or serious, one characteristic stands out: it is tenacity. *Tenacitas vitrix.* Yet history shows that winning is not all that Guardsmen achieve. As if combining oil and water, they manage somehow to combine winning with humanity. In war, that is an extraordinary test of human spirit, requiring great personal belief, dedication and discipline.

On 8th April 1960, Major-General Sir Allan Adair, Baronet, succeeded General The Lord Jeffreys, as Colonel of The Regiment. Small and like Nelson, even diminutive of stature, General Allan exuded infectious humanity and good cheer. As an active, close quarter veteran of both world wars, he inspired both love and devoted loyalty in all ranks, in what can best be described as the 'Nelsonic Manner'. He was a particularly gifted public speaker and reader. His introduction of his, "old friend, Harold Macmillan" as guest speaker at the First Guards Club dinner will be remembered as epic. His reading of the Lesson at Black Sunday Services inspired all who attended. He was, truly, a 'Great Grenadier'.

In the late 1960's General Sir Allan, as 'The Colonel', visited the Guards Depot at Pirbright to inspect 14 Company. As the Second Captain it was my privilege to sit next to him at luncheon. He lived up to his universal reputation as the most charming, inspiring and entertaining of men. Such was his charm that I ventured to ask him what, in his view, set Guardsmen apart. After a moment of thought, he replied that, *"Guardsmen only leave a position on a stretcher."* It was a seminal remark that intrigued me as I continued through life to read more history. In short, it amounted to the fact that 'Guardsmen never give up' or, they always show, in a single word, 'Tenacity.'

Perhaps it is not merely a coincidence that the Great Man who, in the winter of 1941, demanded of us all, as a Nation, that we "Never give in; never, never, never, never give in" followed his own demands in his challenging personal life. In 1915, he was denied a commission in The Regiment on the grounds that The Guards allowed only Guards Officers to command Guardsmen. However, undaunted and tenacious to the end, Winston Churchill (a former Cabinet Minister and a proven veteran of the battle of Omderman) then changed his application to request "an attachment (to the Grenadier Guards) under instruction" (to be taught the ropes of trench warfare). That was an illustration of *tenacitas victrix*. Ironically Winston Churchill, who had gained a commission in the Queen's Own Oxfordshire Hussars, before commanding the 6th

Battalion, the Royal Scots Fusiliers, was attached, in the winter of 1915, to the 2nd (*Elite*) Battalion, Grenadier Guards under Lieutenant-Colonel G. D. Jeffreys. (Evidently, he was so impressed by Colonel 'Ma' that, when Prime Minister, he recommended that Jeffreys be made a Peer of the Realm.) It was the same battalion that Winston Churchill's ancestor John, 1st Duke of Marlborough, commanded some 200 years before. It was also the very same battalion that conducted Sir Winston Churchill's funeral, exactly 50 years later. According to Lord Edward Cecil, Churchill, 'adored the Regiment and would talk all day about it. ...'

It appears, therefore, that it is unquestioned loyalty, magnanimous humanity and total tenacity in battle that most distinguishes Guardsmen.

Finally, how are Grenadiers different from other Guards regiments? In my humble opinion, as all Grenadiers are Guardsmen, there can be precious little spiritual difference between the 'The Tins; Blues; Bill Browns; Lillywhites; Jocks; Micks or the Taffs.' However, history proves that none can say that they exemplify the loyalty, humanity and tenacious fighting spirit of the Guards, more than a British Grenadier!

Afterword

When change descends like a sudden gale
Let my spirit be first to stand and prevail
—Alexandra de Borchgrave

Divorce is often a sad and bitter event. Mine was paraded across the headlines as a great story against a Tory MP. As court records show, my barristers' technical motion to bring the matter back before the Court, was falsely portrayed as an indication that I was trying to imprison my former wife and even that I was claiming alimony. Both these accusations were entirely untrue. The facts were that the High Court, having heard all the evidence on oath, over many days, awarded me not just my Court costs, but all my legal expenses. In addition, the High Court went out of its way to express the view that I had behaved entirely properly throughout the proceedings, and were of the further opinion that I had behaved as a gentleman. The High Court findings were subsequently upheld by the Court of Appeal, which also pointed to the differences between the publicity and the facts. However, these findings and opinions were cynically ignored by the tabloids.

Later, Labour slated the Conservatives as the party of sleaze. I was told that a deal was done in which the Conservatives agreed to offer up the head of a Tory MP in order to get the Socialists to stop. Regardless, I was subjected to what I termed a very public Political 'Show Trial'. I was accused of not declaring overseas payments to my consulting company, which itself was properly declared. I never denied this because I had previously been told not to declare them by the then Registrar. He told me that, as my company was declared, I should not do so. Indeed, he added that, had I declared myself as a director of

233

ICI, to declare the massive, daily overseas payments to that company would "...make a farce of the whole Register." Nevertheless, the Show Trial was established. In keeping with the debased politics of the modern day (leading eventually, perhaps to a new 'Post Democracy' era), it disregarded completely ancient precident. Crucially, it ignored the traditional method of 'trying' a Member of Parliament, before the full House of Lords, acting as Jury, under the Lord Chancellor, as Judge. (Even Mr. Speaker told me: "There's not an ounce of justice in this, John, but it is the unfortunate reality of what you face tomorrow. You will be allowed to make a short but uncontroversial Statement provided you undertake to make no defensive statements, such as arguing with the Select Committee Report, and you must agree not to take any further part in the debate, by asking questions, making interventions or the like.") This long-accepted Parliamentary Court was cynically bypassed by the Tory Government. As 'Hansard' shows, the House of Commons, under the secretive and ruthless control of the Tory Whips, assumed to itself the monopoly legal powers of Investigator, sole Witness (the Select Committee Report), Prosecutor, Judge and (paid) Jury, all without any defence or Right of Appeal. The result was a foregone conclusion: the 'payroll' whipped vote, under the guise of a free vote, ensured conviction and a draconian punishment. I was paraded in front of television and publicly disgraced. In the media frenzy that followed, I was even encouraged to take my own life. Indeed, one tabloid provided instructions as to how to do so.

Some idea of the iniquity of this trial was shown later by the case of The Right Honourable John Major MP, who despite the vivid precedent of my case, had, I am told, apparently failed to declare overseas payments taken, not to a correctly declared company, but, more seriously, directly to himself. However, as a former Tory Prime Minister, I understand he was merely sent a Letter of Reprimand, with the minimum of publicity. Today, the scandal of the secret loans to both the Socialist and Tory parties shows vividly the underlying cynical hypocrisy of the entire issue.

About the Author

Born in Hampshire, John Browne grew up on a family farm near Bath. Educated at Malvern, he entered the Guards Depot at Caterham as a Grenadier recruit in 1957. Upon graduation from the Royal Military Academy Sandhurst in 1959 he was commissioned into the Grenadier Guards. He served in both the 1st and 2nd Battalions and at the Guards Depot. He was posted twice to Germany and to Cyprus and British Guiana.

Later, he undertook postgraduate masters degree studies at Cranfield Institute of Technology (MSc) and at Harvard (MBA). Subsequently, he worked in New York and in London as an investment banker and as a merchant banker, respectively. He was the Conservative Councillor for Knightsbridge on the Westminster City Council from 1974 to 1978. Subsequently he was elected as the Conservative Member of Parliament for Winchester, throughout the Thatcher years. In 1992, facing reselection, he stood as an Independent Conservative (against a Federal Europe) and lost his seat in Parliament. He now works in the financial services industry in America.

He has prepared many of the notes for a book of 100 short stories, entitled *Life's a Laugh (on occasion)* from which these stories are taken. He has prepared a book, ready for publication, entitled, *Tarantula—An Anglo-American Special Forces Hunt for bin Laden*. He is currently writing a romantic historical novel about the Romanovs which, he says, "will have strong Grenadier connections."